QUEEN ELIZABETH

CHAPTER I.

ELIZABETH'S MOTHER.

1533-1536

Greenwich.--The hospital.--Its inmates.--Greenwich Observatory.--Manner of taking time.--Henry the Eighth.--His character.--His six wives.--Anne Boleyn.--Catharine of Aragon.--Henry discards her.--Origin of the English Church.--Henry marries Anne Boleyn.--Birth of Elizabeth.--Ceremony of christening.--Baptism of Elizabeth.--Grand procession.--Train-bearers.--The church.--The silver font.--The presents.--Name of the infant princess.--Elizabeth made Princess of Wales.--Matrimonial schemes.--Jane Seymour.--The tournament.--The king's suspicions.--Queen Anne arrested.--She is sent to the Tower.--Sufferings of the queen.--Her mental distress.--Examination of Anne.--Her letter to the king.--Anne's fellow-prisoners.--They are executed.--Anne tried and condemned.--She protests her innocence.--Anne's execution.--Disposition of the body.--The king's brutality.--Elizabeth's forlorn condition.

Travelers, in ascending the Thames by the steamboat from Rotterdam, on their return from an excursion to the Rhine, have often their attention strongly attracted by what appears to be a splendid palace on the banks of the river at Greenwich. The edifice is not a palace, however, but a hospital, or, rather, a retreat where the worn out, maimed, and crippled veterans of the English navy spend the remnant of their days in comfort and peace, on pensions allowed them by the government in whose service they have spent their strength or lost their limbs. The magnificent buildings of the hospital stand on level land near the river. Behind them there is a beautiful park, which extends over the undulating and rising ground in the rear; and on the summit of one of the eminences there is the famous Greenwich Observatory, on the precision of whose quadrants and micrometers depend those calculations by which the navigation of the world is guided. The most unconcerned and careless spectator is interested in the manner in which the ships which throng the river all the way from Greenwich to London, "take their time" from this observatory before setting sail for distant seas. From the top of a cupola surmounting the edifice, a slender pole ascends, with a black ball upon it, so constructed as to slide up and down for a few feet upon the pole. When the hour of 12 M. approaches, the ball slowly rises to within a few inches of the top, warning the ship-masters in the river to be ready with their chronometers, to observe and note the precise instant of its fall. When a few seconds only remain of the time, the ball ascends the remainder of the distance by a very deliberate motion, and then drops suddenly when the instant arrives. The ships depart on their several destinations, and for months afterward when thousands of miles away they depend for their safety in dark and stormy nights, and among dangerous reefs and rocky shores, on the nice approximation to correctness in the note of time which this descending ball had given them.

This is Greenwich, as it exists at the present day. At the time when the events occurred which are to be related in this narrative, it was most known on account of a royal palace which was situated there. This palace was the residence of the then queen consort of England. The king reigning at that time was Henry the Eighth. He was an unprincipled and cruel tyrant, and the chief business of his life seemed to be selecting and marrying new queens, making room for each succeeding one by discarding, divorcing, or beheading her predecessor. There were six of them in all, and, with one exception, the history of each one is a distinct and separate, but dreadful tragedy. As there were so many of them, and they figured as queens each for so short a period, they are commonly designated in history by their personal family names, and even in these names there is a great similarity. There were three Catharines, two Annes, and a Jane. The only one who lived and died in peace, respected and beloved to the end, was the Jane.

Queen Elizabeth, the subject of this narrative, was the daughter of the second wife in this strange succession, and her mother was one of the Annes. Her name in full was Anne Boleyn. She was young and very beautiful, and Henry, to prepare the way for making her his wife, divorced his first queen, or rather declared his marriage with her null and void, because she had been, before he married her, the wife of his brother. Her name was Catharine of Aragon. She was, while connected with him, a faithful, true, and affectionate wife. She was a Catholic. The Catholic rules are very strict in respect to the marriage of relatives, and a special dispensation from the pope was necessary to authorize marriage in such a case as that of Henry and Catharine. This dispensation had, however, been obtained, and Catharine had, in reliance upon it, consented to become Henry's wife. When, however, she was no longer young and beautiful, and Henry had become enamored of Anne Boleyn, who was so, he discarded Catharine, and espoused the beautiful girl in her stead. He wished the pope to annul his dispensation, which would, of course, annul the marriage; and because the pontiff refused, and all the efforts of Henry's government were unavailing to move him, he abandoned the Catholic faith, and established an independent Protestant church in England, whose supreme authority would annul the marriage. Thus, in a great measure, came the Reformation in England. The Catholics reproach us, and, it must be confessed, with some justice, with the ignominiousness of its origin.

The course which things thus took created a great deal of delay in the formal annulling of the marriage with Catharine, which Henry was too impatient and imperious to bear. He would not wait for the decree of divorce, but took Anne Boleyn for his wife before his previous connection was made void. He said he was privately married to her. This he had, as he maintained, a right to do, for he considered his first marriage as void, absolutely and of itself, without any decree. When, at length, the decree was finally passed, he brought Anne Boleyn forward as his queen, and introduced her as such to England and to the world by a genuine marriage and a most magnificent coronation. The people of England pitied poor Catharine, but they joined very cordially, notwithstanding, in welcoming the youthful and beautiful lady who was to take her place. All London gave itself up to festivities and rejoicings on the occasion of these nuptials. Immediately after this the young queen retired to her palace in Greenwich, and in two or three months afterward little Elizabeth was born. Her birth-day was the 7th of September, 1533.

The mother may have loved the babe, but Henry himself was sadly disappointed that his child was not a son. Notwithstanding her sex, however, she was a personage of great distinction from her very birth, as all the realm looked upon her as heir to the crown. Henry was himself, at this time, very fond of Anne Boleyn, though his feelings afterward were entirely changed. He determined on giving to the infant a very splendid christening. The usage in the Church of England is to make the christening of a child not merely a solemn religious ceremony, but a great festive occasion of congratulations and rejoicing. The unconscious subject of the ceremony is taken to the church. Certain near and distinguished friends, gentlemen and ladies, appear as godfathers and godmothers, as they are termed, to the child. They, in the ceremony, are considered as presenting the infant for consecration to Christ, and as becoming responsible for its future initiation into the Christian faith. They are hence sometimes called sponsors. These sponsors are supposed to take, from the time of the baptism forward, a strong interest in all that pertains to the welfare of their little charge, and they usually manifest this interest by presents on the day of the christening. These things are all conducted with considerable ceremony and parade in ordinary cases, occurring in private life; and when a princess is to be baptized, all, even the most minute details of the ceremony, assume a great importance, and the whole scene becomes one of great pomp and splendor.

The babe, in this case, was conveyed to the church in a grand procession. The mayor and other civic authorities in London came down to Greenwich in barges, tastefully ornamented, to join in the ceremony. The lords and ladies of King Henry's court were also there, in attendance at the palace. When all were assembled, and every thing was ready, the procession moved from the palace to the church with great pomp. The road, all the way, was carpeted with green rushes, spread upon the ground. Over this road the little infant was borne by one of her godmothers. She was wrapped in a mantle of purple velvet, with a long train appended to it, which was trimmed with ermine, a very costly kind of fur, used in England as a badge of authority. This train was borne by lords and ladies of high rank, who were appointed for the purpose by the king, and who deemed their office a very distinguished honor. Besides these train-bearers, there were four lords, who walked two on each side of the child, and who held over her a magnificent canopy. Other personages of high rank and station followed, bearing various insignia and emblems, such as by the ancient customs of England are employed on these occasions, and all dressed sumptuously in gorgeous robes, and wearing the badges and decorations pertaining to their rank or the offices they held. Vast crowds of spectators lined the way, and gazed upon the scene.

On arriving at the church, they found the interior splendidly decorated for the occasion. Its walls were lined throughout with tapestry, and in the center was a crimson canopy, under which was placed a large silver font, containing the water with which the child was to be baptized. The ceremony was performed by Cranmer, the archbishop of Canterbury, which is the office of the highest dignitary of the English Church. After it was performed, the procession returned as it came, only now there was an addition of four persons of high rank, who followed the child with the presents intended for her by the godfathers and godmothers. These presents consisted of cups and bowls, of beautiful workmanship, some of silver gilt, and some of solid gold. They were very costly, though not prized much yet by the unconscious infant for whom they were intended. She went and came, in the midst of this gay and joyous procession, little imagining into what a restless and unsatisfying life all this pageantry and splendor were ushering her.

They named the child Elizabeth, from her grandmother. There have been many queens of that name, but Queen Elizabeth of England became so much more distinguished than any other, that that name alone has become her usual designation. Her family name was Tudor. As she was never married--for, though her life was one perpetual scene of matrimonial schemes and negotiations, she lived and died a maiden lady--she has been sometimes called the Virgin Queen, and one of the states of this Union, Virginia, receives its name from this designation of Elizabeth. She is also often familiarly called Queen Bess.

Making little Elizabeth presents of gold and silver plate, and arranging splendid pageants for her, were not the only plans for her aggrandizement which were formed during the period of her infantile unconsciousness. The king, her father, first had an act of Parliament passed, solemnly recognizing and confirming her claim as heir to the crown, and the title of Princess of Wales was formally conferred upon her. When these things were done, Henry began to consider how he could best promote his own political schemes by forming an engagement of marriage for her, and, when she was only about two years of age, he offered her to the King of France as the future wife of one of his sons, on certain conditions of political service which he wished him to perform. But the King of France would not accede to the terms, and so this plan was abandoned. Elizabeth was, however, notwithstanding this failure, an object of universal interest and attention, as the daughter of a very powerful monarch, and the heir to his crown. Her life opened with very bright and serene prospects of future greatness; but all these prospects were soon apparently cut off by a very heavy cloud which arose to darken her sky. This cloud was the sudden and dreadful fall and ruin of her mother.

Queen Anne Boleyn was originally a maid of honor to Queen Catharine, and became acquainted with King Henry and gained his affections while she was acting in that capacity. When she became queen herself, she had, of course, her own maids of honor, and among them was one named Jane Seymour. Jane was a beautiful and accomplished lady, and in the end she supplanted her mistress and queen in Henry's affections, just as Anne herself had supplanted Catharine. The king had removed Catharine to make way for Anne, by annulling his marriage with her on account of their relationship: what way could he contrive now to remove Anne, so as to make way for Jane?

He began to entertain, or to pretend to entertain, feelings of jealousy and suspicion that Anne was unfaithful to him. One day, at a sort of tournament in the park of the royal palace at Greenwich, when a great crowd of gayly-dressed ladies and gentlemen were assembled to witness the spectacle, the queen dropped her handkerchief. A gentleman whom the king had suspected of being one of her favorites picked it up. He did not immediately restore it to her. There was, besides, something in the air and manner of the gentleman, and in the attendant circumstances of the case, which the king's mind seized upon as evidence of criminal gallantry between the parties. He was, or at least pretended to be, in a great rage. He left the field immediately and went to London. The tournament was broken up in confusion, the queen was seized by the king's orders, conveyed to her palace in Greenwich, and shut up in her chamber, with a lady who had always been her rival and enemy to guard her. She was in great consternation and sorrow, but she declared most solemnly that she was innocent of any crime, and had always been true and faithful to the king.

The next day she was taken from her palace at Greenwich up the river, probably in a barge well guarded by armed men, to the Tower of London. The Tower is an ancient and very extensive castle, consisting of a great number of buildings inclosed within a high wall. It is in the lower part of London, on the bank of the Thames, with a flight of stairs leading down to the river from a great postern gate. The unhappy queen was landed at these stairs and conveyed into the castle, and shut up in a gloomy apartment, with walls of stone and windows barricaded with strong bars of iron. There were four or five gentlemen, attendants upon the queen in her palace at Greenwich, whom the king suspected, or pretended to suspect, of being her accomplices in crime, that were arrested at the same time with her and closely confined.

When the poor queen was introduced into her dungeon, she fell on her knees, and, in an agony of terror and despair, she implored God to help her in this hour of her extremity, and most solemnly called him to witness that she was innocent of the crime imputed to her charge. Seeking thus a refuge in God calmed and composed her in some small degree; but when, again, thoughts of the imperious and implacable temper of her husband came over her, of the impetuousness of his passions, of the certainty that he wished her removed out of the way in order that room might be made for her rival, and then, when her distracted mind turned to the forlorn and helpless condition of her little daughter Elizabeth, now scarcely three years old, her fortitude and self-possession forsook her entirely; she sank half insane upon her bed, in long and uncontrollable paroxysms of sobs and tears, alternating with still more uncontrollable and frightful bursts of hysterical laughter.

The king sent a commission to take her examination. At the same time, he urged her, by the persons whom he sent, to confess her guilt, promising her that, if she did so, her life should be spared. She, however, protested her innocence with the utmost firmness and constancy. She begged earnestly to be allowed to see the king, and, when this was refused, she wrote a letter to him, which still remains, and which expresses very strongly the acuteness of her mental sufferings.

In this letter, she said that she was so distressed and bewildered by the king's displeasure and her imprisonment, that she hardly knew what to think or to say. She assured him that she had always been faithful and true to him, and begged that he would not cast an indelible stain upon her own fair fame and that of her innocent and helpless child by such unjust and groundless imputations. She begged him to let her have a fair trial by impartial persons, who would weigh the evidence against her in a just and equitable manner. She was sure that by this course her innocence would be established, and he himself, and all mankind would see that she had been most unjustly accused.

But if, on the other hand, she added, the king had determined on her destruction, in order to remove an obstacle in the way of his possession of a new object of love, she prayed that God would forgive him and all her enemies for so great a sin, and not call him to account for it at the last day. She urged him, at all events, to spare the lives of the four gentlemen who had been accused, as she assured him they were wholly innocent of the crime laid to their charge, begging him, if he had ever loved the name of Anne Boleyn, to grant this her last request. She signed her letter his "most loyal and ever faithful wife," and dated it from her "doleful prison in the Tower."

The four gentlemen were promised that their lives should be spared if they would confess their guilt. One of them did, accordingly, admit his guilt, and the others persisted to the end in firmly denying it. They who think Anne Boleyn was innocent, suppose that the one who confessed did it as the most likely mode of averting destruction, as men have often been known, under the influence of fear, to confess crimes of which it was afterward proved they could not have been guilty. If this was his motive, it was of no avail. The four persons accused, after a very informal trial, in which nothing was really proved against them, were condemned, apparently to please the king, and were executed together.

Three days after this the queen herself was brought to trial before the peers. The number of peers of the realm in England at this time was fifty-three. Only twenty-six were present at the trial. The king is charged with making such arrangements as to prevent the attendance of those who would be unwilling to pass sentence of condemnation. At any rate, those who did attend professed to be satisfied of the guilt of the accused, and they sentenced her to be burned, or to be beheaded, at the pleasure of the king. He decided that she should be beheaded.

The execution was to take place in a little green area within the Tower. The platform was erected here, and the block placed upon it, the whole being covered with a black cloth, as usual on such occasions. On the morning of the fatal day, Anne sent for the constable of the Tower to come in and receive her dying protestations that she was innocent of the crimes alleged against her. She told him that she understood that she was not to die until 12 o'clock, and that she was sorry for it, for she wished to have it over. The constable told her the pain would be very slight and momentary. "Yes," she rejoined, "I am told that a very skillful executioner is provided, and my neck is very slender."

At the appointed hour she was led out into the court-yard where the execution was to take place. There were about twenty persons present, all officers of state or of the city of London. The bodily suffering attendant upon the execution was very soon over, for the slender neck was severed at a single blow, and probably all sensibility to pain immediately ceased. Still, the lips and the eyes were observed to move and quiver for a few seconds after the separation of the head from the body. It was a relief, however, to the spectators when this strange and unnatural prolongation of the mysterious functions of life came to an end.

No coffin had been provided. They found, however, an old wooden chest, made to contain arrows, lying in one of the apartments of the tower, which they used instead. They first laid the decapitated trunk within it, and then adjusted the dissevered head to its place, as if vainly attempting to repair the irretrievable injury they had done. They hurried the body, thus enshrined, to its burial in a chapel, which was also within the tower, doing all with such dispatch that the whole was finished before the clock struck twelve; and the next day the unfeeling monster who was the author of this dreadful deed was publicly married to his new favorite, Jane Seymour.

The king had not merely procured Anne's personal condemnation; he had also obtained a decree annulling his marriage with her, on the ground of her having been, as he attempted to prove, previously affianced to another man. This was, obviously, a mere pretense. The object was to cut off Elizabeth's rights to inherit the crown, by making his marriage with her mother void. Thus was the little princess left motherless and friendless when only three years old.

CHAPTER II.

THE CHILDHOOD OF A PRINCESS.

1536-1548

Elizabeth's condition at the death of her mother.--Her residence.--Letter of Lady Bryan, Elizabeth's governess.--Conclusion of letter.--Troubles and trials of infancy.--Birth of Edward.--The king reconciled to his daughters.--Death of King Henry.--His children.--King Henry's violence.--The order of succession.--Elizabeth's troubles.--The two Seymours.--The queen dowager's marriage.--The Seymours quarrel.--Somerset's power and influence.--Jealousies and quarrels.--Mary Queen of Scots.--Marriage schemes.--Seymour's promotion.--Jane Grey.--Family quarrels.--Death of the queen dowager.--Seymour's schemes.--Seymour's arrest.--His trial and attainder.--Seymour beheaded.--

Elizabeth's trials.--Elizabeth's firmness.--Lady Tyrwhitt.--Elizabeth's sufferings.--Her fidelity to her friends.

Elizabeth was about three years old at the death of her mother. She was a princess, but she was left in a very forlorn and desolate condition. She was not, however, entirely abandoned. Her claims to inherit the crown had been set aside, but then she was, as all admitted, the daughter of the king, and she must, of course, be the object of a certain degree of consideration and ceremony. It would be entirely inconsistent with the notions of royal dignity which then prevailed to have her treated like an ordinary child.

She had a residence assigned her at a place called Hunsdon, and was put under the charge of a governess whose name was Lady Bryan. There is an ancient letter from Lady Bryan, still extant, which was written to one of the king's officers about Elizabeth, explaining her destitute condition, and asking for a more suitable supply for her wants. It may entertain the reader to see this relic, which not only illustrates our little heroine's condition, but also shows how great the changes are which our language has undergone within the last three hundred years. The letter, as here given, is abridged a little from the original:

My Lord:

When your Lordship was last here, it pleased you to say that I should not be mistrustful of the King's Grace, nor of your Lordship, which word was of great comfort to me, and emboldeneth me now to speak my poor mind.

Now so it is, my Lord, that my Lady Elizabeth is put from the degree she was afore, and what degree she is at now[A] I know not but by hearsay. Therefore I know not how to order her, nor myself, nor none of hers that I have the rule of--that is, her women and her grooms. But I beseech you to be good, my Lord, to her and to all hers, and to let her have some rayment; for she has neither gown, nor kirtle, nor no manner of linen, nor foresmocks, nor kerchiefs, nor sleeves, nor rails, nor bodystitchets, nor mufflers, nor biggins. All these her Grace's wants I have driven off as long as I can, by my troth, but I can not any longer. Beseeching you, my Lord, that you will see that her Grace may have that is needful for her, and that I may know from you, in writing, how I shall order myself towards her, and whatever is the King's Grace's pleasure and yours, in every thing, that I shall do.

[Footnote A: That is, in what light the king and the government wish to have her regarded, and how they wish her to be treated.]

My Lord Mr. Shelton would have my Lady Elizabeth to dine and sup at the board of estate. Alas, my Lord, it is not meet for a child of her age to keep such rule yet. I promise you, my Lord, I dare not take upon me to keep her in health and she keep that rule; for there she shall see divers meats and fruits, and wines, which would be hard for me to restrain her Grace from it. You know, my Lord, there is no place of correction[B] there, and she is yet too young to correct greatly. I know well, and she be there, I shall never bring her up to the King's Grace's honor nor hers, nor to her health, nor my poor honesty. Wherefore, I beseech you, my Lord, that my Lady may have a mess of meat to her own lodging, with a good dish or two that is meet for her Grace to eat of.

[Footnote B: That is, opportunity for correction.]

My Lady hath likewise great pain with her teeth, and they come very slowly forth, and this causeth me to suffer her Grace to have her will more than I would. I trust to God, and her teeth were well graft, to have her Grace after another fashion than she is yet, so as I trust the King's Grace shall have great comfort in her Grace; for she is as toward a child, and as gentle of conditions, as ever I knew any in my life. Jesu preserve her Grace.

Good my Lord, have my Lady's Grace, and us that be her poor servants, in your remembrance.

This letter evinces that strange mixture of state and splendor with discomfort and destitution, which prevailed very extensively in royal households in those early times. A part of the privation which Elizabeth seems, from this letter, to have endured, was doubtless owing to the rough manners of the day; but there is no doubt that she was also, at least for a time, in a neglected and forsaken condition. The new queen, Jane Seymour, who succeeded Elizabeth's mother, had a son a year or two after her marriage. He was named Edward. Thus Henry had three children, Mary, Elizabeth, and Edward, each one the child of a different wife; and the last of them, the son, appears to have monopolized, for a time, the king's affection and care.

Still, the hostility which the king had felt for these queens in succession was owing, as has been already said, to his desire to remove them out of his way, that he might be at liberty to marry again; and so, after the mothers were, one after another, removed, the hostility itself, so far as the children were concerned, gradually subsided, and the king began to look both upon Mary and Elizabeth with favor again. He even formed plans for marrying Elizabeth to persons of distinction in foreign countries, and he entered into some negotiations for this purpose. He had a decree passed, too, at last, reversing the sentence by which the two princesses were cut off from an inheritance of the crown. Thus they were restored, during their father's life, to their proper rank as royal princesses.

At last the king died in 1547, leaving only these three children, each one the child of a different wife. Mary was a maiden lady, of about thirty-one years of age. She was a stern, austere, hard-hearted woman, whom nobody loved. She was the daughter of King Henry's first wife, Catharine of Aragon, and, like her mother, was a decided Catholic.

Next came Elizabeth, who was about fourteen years of age. She was the daughter of the king's second wife, Queen Anne Boleyn. She had been educated a Protestant. She was not pretty, but was a very lively and sprightly child, altogether different in her cast of character and in her manners from her sister Mary.

Then, lastly, there was Edward, the son of Jane Seymour, the third queen. He was about nine years of age at his father's death. He was a boy of good character, mild and gentle in his disposition, fond of study and reflection, and a general favorite with all who knew him.

It was considered in those days that a king might, in some sense, dispose of his crown by will, just as, at the present time, a man may bequeath his house or his farm. Of course, there were some limits to this power, and the concurrence of Parliament seems to have been required to the complete validity of such a settlement. King Henry the Eighth, however, had little difficulty in carrying any law through Parliament which he desired to have enacted. It is said that, on one occasion, when there was some delay about passing a bill of his, he sent for one of the most influential of the members of the House of Commons to come into his presence. The member came and kneeled before him. "Ho, man!" said the king, "and will they not suffer my bill to pass?" He then came up and put his hand upon the kneeling legislator's head, and added, "Get my bill passed to-morrow, or else by to-morrow this head of yours shall be off." The next day the bill was passed accordingly.

King Henry, before he died, arranged the order of succession to the throne as follows: Edward was to succeed him; but, as he was a minor, being then only nine years of age, a great council of state, consisting of sixteen persons of the highest rank, was appointed to govern the kingdom in his name until he should be eighteen years of age, when he was to become king in reality as well as in name. In case he should die without heirs, then Mary, his oldest sister, was to succeed him; and if she died without heirs, then Elizabeth was to succeed her. This arrangement went into full effect. The council governed the kingdom in Edward's name until he was sixteen years of age, when he died. Then Mary followed, and reigned as queen five years longer, and died without children, and during all this time Elizabeth held the rank of a princess, exposed to a thousand difficulties and dangers from the plots, intrigues and conspiracies of those about her, in which, on account of her peculiar position and prospects, she was necessarily involved.

One of the worst of these cases occurred soon after her father's death. There were two brothers of Jane Seymour, who were high in King Henry's favor at the time of his decease. The oldest is known in history by his title of the Earl of Hertford at first, and afterward by that of Duke of Somerset. The youngest was called Sir Thomas Seymour. They were both made members of the government which was to administer the affairs of state during young Edward's minority. They were not, however, satisfied with any moderate degree of power. Being brothers of Jane Seymour, who was Edward's mother, they were his uncles, of course, and the oldest one soon succeeded in causing himself to be appointed protector. By this office he was, in fact, king, all except in name.

The younger brother, who was an agreeable and accomplished man, paid his addresses to the queen dowager, that is, to the widow whom King Henry left, for the last of his wives was living at the time of his death. She consented to marry him, and the marriage took place almost immediately after the king's death--so soon in fact, that it was considered extremely hasty and unbecoming. This queen dowager had two houses left to her, one at Chelsea, and the other at Hanworth, towns some little distance up the river from London. Here she resided with her new husband, sometimes at one of the houses, and sometimes at the other. The king had also directed, in his will, that the Princess Elizabeth should be under her care, so that Elizabeth, immediately after her father's death, lived at one or the other of these two houses under the care of Seymour, who, from having been her uncle, became now, in some sense, her father. He was a sort of uncle, for he was the brother of one of her father's wives. He was a sort of father, for he was the husband of another of them. Yet, really, by blood, there was no relation between them.

The two brothers, Somerset and Seymour, quarreled. Each was very ambitious, and very jealous of the other. Somerset, in addition to being appointed protector by the council, got a grant of power from the young king called a patent. This commission was executed with great formality, and was sealed with the great seal of state, and it made Somerset, in some measure independent of the other nobles whom King Henry had associated with him in the government. By this patent he was placed in supreme command of all the forces by land and sea. He had a seat on the right hand of the throne, under the great canopy of state, and whenever he went abroad on public occasions, he assumed all the pomp and parade which would have been expected in a real king. Young Edward was wholly under his influence, and did always whatever Somerset recommended him to do. Seymour was very jealous of all this greatness, and was contriving every means in his power to circumvent and supersede his brother.

The wives, too, of these great statesmen quarreled. The Duchess of Somerset thought she was entitled to the precedence, because she was the wife of the protector, who, being a kind of regent, she thought he was entitled to have his wife considered as a sort of queen. The wife of Seymour, on the other hand, contended that she was entitled to the precedence as a real queen, having been herself the actual consort of a reigning monarch. The two ladies disputed perpetually on this point, which, of course, could never be settled. They enlisted, however, on their respective sides various partisans, producing a great deal of jealousy and ill will, and increasing the animosity of their husbands.

All this time the celebrated Mary Queen of Scots was an infant in Janet Sinclair's arms, at the castle of Stirling, in Scotland. King Henry, during his life, had made a treaty with the government of Scotland, by which it was agreed that Mary should be married to his son Edward as soon as the two children should have grown to maturity; but afterward, the government of Scotland having fallen from Protestant into Catholic hands, they determined that this match must be given up. The English authorities were very much incensed. They wished to have the marriage take effect, as it would end in uniting the Scotch and English kingdoms; and the protector, when a time arrived which he thought was favorable for his purpose, raised an army and marched northward to make war upon Scotland, and compel the Scots to fulfill the contract of marriage.

While his brother was gone to the northward, Seymour remained at home, and endeavored, by every means within his reach, to strengthen his own influence and increase his power. He contrived to obtain from the council of government the office of lord high admiral, which gave him the command of the fleet, and made him, next to his brother, the most powerful and important personage in the realm. He had, besides, as has already been stated, the custody and care of Elizabeth, who lived in his house; though, as he was a profligate and unprincipled man, this position for the princess, now fast growing up to womanhood, was considered by many persons as of doubtful propriety. Still, she was at present only fourteen years old. There was another young lady likewise in his family, a niece of King Henry, and, of course, a second cousin of Elizabeth. Her name was Jane Grey. It was a very unhappy family. The manners and habits of all the members of it, excepting Jane Grey, seem to have been very rude and irregular. The admiral quarreled with his wife, and was jealous of the very servants who waited upon her. The queen observed something in the manners of her husband toward the young princess which made her angry both with him and her. Elizabeth resented this, and a violent quarrel ensued, which ended in their separation. Elizabeth went away, and resided afterward at a place called Hatfield.

Very soon after this, the queen dowager died suddenly. People accused Seymour, her husband, of having poisoned her, in order to make way for the Princess Elizabeth to be his wife. He denied this, but he immediately began to lay his plans for securing the hand of Elizabeth. There was a probability that she might, at some future time, succeed to the crown, and then, if he were her husband, he thought he should be the real sovereign, reigning in her name.

Elizabeth had in her household two persons, a certain Mrs. Ashley, who was then her governess, and a man named Parry, who was a sort of treasurer. He was called the cofferer. The admiral gained these persons over to his interests, and, through them, attempted to open communications with Elizabeth, and persuade her to enter into his designs. Of course, the whole affair was managed with great secrecy. They were all liable to a charge of treason against the government of Edward by such plots, as his ministers and counselors might maintain that their design was to overthrow Edward's government and make Elizabeth queen. They, therefore, were all banded together to keep their councils secret, and Elizabeth was drawn, in some degree, into the scheme, though precisely how far was never fully known. It was supposed that she began to love Seymour, although he was very much older than herself, and to be willing to become his wife. It is not surprising that, neglected and forsaken as she had been, she should have been inclined to regard with favor an agreeable and influential man, who expressed a strong affection for her, and a warm interest in her welfare.

However this may be, Elizabeth was one day struck with consternation at hearing that Seymour was arrested by order of his brother, who had returned from Scotland and had received information of his designs, and that he had been committed to the Tower. He had a hurried and irregular trial, or what, in those days, was called a trial. The council went themselves to the Tower, and had him brought before them and examined. He demanded to have the charges made out in form, and the witnesses confronted with him, but the council were satisfied of his guilt without these formalities. The Parliament immediately afterward passed a bill of attainder against him, by which he was sentenced to death. His brother, the protector, signed the warrant for his execution, and he was beheaded on Tower Hill.

The protector sent two messengers in the course of this affair to Elizabeth, to see what they could ascertain from her about it. Sir Robert Tyrwhitt was the name of the principal one of these messengers. When the cofferer learned that they were at the gate, he went in great terror into his chamber, and said that he was undone. At the same time, he pulled off a chain from his neck, and the rings from his fingers, and threw them away from him with gesticulations of despair. The messengers then came to Elizabeth, and told her, falsely as it seems, with a view to frighten her into confessions, that Mrs. Ashley and the cofferer were both secured and sent to the Tower. She seemed very much alarmed; she wept bitterly, and it was a long time before she regained her composure. She wanted to know whether they had confessed any thing. The protector's messengers would not tell her this, but they urged her to confess herself all that had occurred; for, whatever it was, they said that the evil and shame would all be ascribed to the other persons concerned, and not to her, on account of her youth and inexperience. But Elizabeth would confess nothing. The messengers went away, convinced, as they said, that she was guilty; they could see that in her countenance; and that her silence was owing to her firm determination not to betray her lover. They sent word to the protector that they did not believe that any body would succeed in drawing the least information from her, unless it was the protector, or young King Edward himself.

These mysterious circumstances produced a somewhat unfavorable impression in regard to Elizabeth, and there were some instances, it was said, of light and trifling behavior between Elizabeth and Seymour, while she was in his house during the life-time of his wife. They took place in the presence of Seymour's wife, and seem of no consequence, except to show that dukes and princesses got into frolics sometimes in those days as well as other mortals. People censured Mrs. Ashley for not enjoining a greater dignity and propriety of demeanor in her young charge, and the government removed her from her place.

Lady Tyrwhitt, who was the wife of the messenger referred to above that was sent to examine Elizabeth, was appointed to succeed Mrs. Ashley. Elizabeth was very much displeased at this change. She told Lady Tyrwhitt that Mrs. Ashley was her mistress, and that she had not done any thing to make it necessary for the council to put more mistresses over her. Sir Robert wrote to the protector that she took the affair so heavily that she "wept all night, and lowered all the next day." He said that her attachment to Mrs. Ashley was very strong; and that, if any thing were said against the lord admiral, she could not bear to hear it, but took up his defense in the most prompt and eager manner.

How far it is true that Elizabeth loved the unfortunate Seymour can now never be known. There is no doubt, however, but that this whole affair was a very severe trial and affliction to her. It came upon her when she was but fourteen or fifteen years of age, and when she was in a position, as well of an age, which renders the heart acutely sensitive both to the effect of kindness and of injuries. Seymour, by his death, was lost to her forever, and Elizabeth lived in great retirement and seclusion during the remainder of her brother's reign. She did not, however, forget Mrs. Ashley and Parry. On her accession to the throne, many years afterward, she gave them offices very valuable, considering their station in life, and was a true friend to them both to the end of their days.

CHAPTER III.

LADY JANE GREY.

1550-1553

Lady Jane Grey.--Her disposition and character.--Lady Jane's parents.--Restraints put upon her.--Lady Jane's attainments.--Character of her teacher.--Anecdote of Elizabeth and Aylmer.--Lady Jane's attachment to Aylmer.--Elizabeth's studies.--Roger Ascham.--Lady Jane's acquirements in Greek.--Her interview with Ascham.--Lady Jane's intimacy with Edward.--The Earl of Northumberland.--Harsh treatment of Mary.--Decline of Edward's health.--Uncertainty in respect to the succession.--Struggle for power.--Queen Elizabeth's family connections.--Explanation of the table.--King Henry's will.--Various claimants for the throne.--Perplexing questions.--Power of Northumberland.--His schemes.--Marriage of Lady Jane.--Feelings of the people.--Efforts to set Mary aside.--Northumberland works on the young king.--Conduct of the judges.--Pardon by anticipation.--Edward's deed of settlement.--Plan to entrap the princesses.--Death of Edward.--Escape of the princesses.--Precautions of Mary.--Lady Jane proclaimed queen.--Great excitement.--Public opinion in favor of Mary.--Northumberland taken prisoner.--He is beheaded.--Mary's triumphal procession.--Shared by Elizabeth.

Among Elizabeth's companions and playmates in her early years was a young lady, her cousin, as she was often called, though she was really the daughter of her cousin, named Jane Grey, commonly called in history Lady Jane Grey. Her mother was the Marchioness of Dorset, and was the daughter of one of King Henry the Eighth's sisters. King Henry had named her as the next in the order of succession after his own children, that is, after Edward his son, and Mary and Elizabeth his two daughters; and, consequently, though she was very young, yet, as she might one day be Queen of England, she was a personage of considerable importance. She was, accordingly, kept near the court, and shared, in some respects, the education and the studies of the two princesses.

Lady Jane was about four years younger than the Princess Elizabeth, and the sweetness of her disposition, united with an extraordinary intellectual superiority, which showed itself at a very early period, made her a universal favorite. Her father and mother, the Marquis and Marchioness of Dorset, lived at an estate they possessed, called Broadgate, in Leicestershire, which is in the central part of England, although they took their title from the county of Dorset, which is on the southwestern coast. They were very proud of their daughter, and attached infinite importance to her descent from Henry VII., and to the possibility that she might one day succeed to the English throne. They were very strict and severe in their manners, and paid great attention to etiquette and punctilio, as persons who are ambitious of rising in the world are very apt to do. In all ages of the world, and among all nations, those who have long been accustomed to a high position are easy and unconstrained in their manners and demeanor, while those who have been newly advanced from a lower station, or who are anticipating or aspiring to such an advance, make themselves slaves to the rules of etiquette and ceremony. It was thus that the father and mother of Lady Jane, anticipating that she might one day become a queen, watched and guarded her incessantly, subjected her to a thousand unwelcome restraints, and repressed all the spontaneous and natural gayety and sprightliness which belongs properly to such a child.

She became, however, a very excellent scholar in consequence of this state of things. She had a private teacher, a man of great eminence for his learning and abilities, and yet of a very kind and gentle spirit, which enabled him to gain a strong hold on his pupil's affection and regard. His name was John Aylmer. The Marquis of Dorset, Lady Jane's father, became acquainted with Mr. Aylmer when he was quite young, and appointed him, when he had finished his education, to come and reside in his family as chaplain and tutor to his children. Aylmer afterward became a distinguished man, was made Bishop of

London, and held many high offices of state under Queen Elizabeth, when she came to reign. He became very much attached to Queen Elizabeth in the middle and latter part of his life, as he had been to Lady Jane in the early part of it. A curious incident occurred during the time that he was in the service of Elizabeth, which illustrates the character of the man. The queen was suffering from the toothache, and it was necessary that the tooth should be extracted. The surgeon was ready with his instruments, and several ladies and gentlemen of the royal household were in the queen's room commiserating her sufferings; but the queen dreaded the operation so excessively that she could not summon fortitude enough to submit to it. Aylmer, after trying some time in vain to encourage her, took his seat in the chair instead of her, and said to the surgeon, "I am an old man, and have but few teeth to lose; but come, draw this one, and let her majesty see how light a matter it is." One would not have supposed that Elizabeth would have allowed this to be done; but she did, and, finding that Aylmer made so light of the operation, she submitted to have it performed upon herself.

But to return to Lady Jane. She was very strongly attached to her teacher, and made great progress in the studies which he arranged for her. Ladies of high rank, in those days, were accustomed to devote great attention to the ancient and modern languages. There was, in fact, a great necessity then, as indeed there is now, for a European princess to be acquainted with the principal languages of Europe; for the various royal families were continually intermarrying with each other, which led to a great many visits, and other intercourse between the different courts. There was also a great deal of intercourse with the pope, in which the Latin language was the medium of communication. Lady Jane devoted a great deal of time to all these studies, and made rapid proficiency in them all.

The Princess Elizabeth was also an excellent scholar. Her teacher was a very learned and celebrated man, named Roger Ascham. She spoke French and Italian as fluently as she did English. She also wrote and spoke Latin with correctness and readiness. She made considerable progress in Greek too. She could write the Greek character very beautifully, and could express herself tolerably well in conversation in that language. One of her companions, a young lady of the name of Cecil, is said to have spoken Greek as well as English. Roger Ascham took great interest in advancing the princess in these studies, and in the course of these his instructions he became acquainted with Lady Jane, and he praises very highly, in his letters, the industry and assiduity of Lady Jane in similar pursuits.

One day Roger Ascham, being on a journey from the north of England to London, stopped to make a call at the mansion of the Marquis of Dorset. He found that the family were all away; they had gone off upon a hunting excursion in the park. Lady Jane, however, had been left at home, and Ascham went in to see her. He found her in the library reading Greek. Ascham examined her a little, and was very much surprised to find how well acquainted with the language she had become, although she was then only about fifteen years old. He told her that he should like very much to have her write him a letter in Greek, and this she readily promised to do. He asked her, also, how it happened that, at her age, she had made such advances in learning. "I will tell you," said she, "how it has happened. One of the greatest benefits that God ever conferred upon me was in giving me so sharp and severe parents and so gentle a teacher; for, when I am in the presence of either my father or mother, whether I speak, keep silence, sit, stand, or go; eat, drink, be merry or sad; be sewing, playing, dancing, or doing any thing else, I must do it, as it were, in just such weight, measure, and number, as perfectly as possible, or else I am so sharply taunted, so cruelly threatened, yea, presently, sometimes with pinches, nips, and bobs, and other ways, which I will not name for the honor I bear my parents, that I am continually teased and tormented. And then, when the time comes for me to go to Mr. Aylmer, he teaches me so gently, so pleasantly, and with such fair allurements to learning, that I think all the time nothing while I am with him; and I am always sorry to go away from him, because whatsoever else I do but learning is full of grief, trouble, fear, and suffering."

Lady Jane Grey was an intimate friend and companion of the young King Edward as long as he lived. Edward died when he was sixteen years of age, so that he did not reach the period which his father had assigned for his reigning in his own name. One of King Edward's most prominent and powerful ministers during the latter part of his life was the Earl of Northumberland. The original name of the Earl of Northumberland was John Dudley. He was one of the train who came in the procession at the close of the baptism of Elizabeth, carrying the presents. He was a Protestant, and was very friendly to Edward and to Lady Jane Grey, for they were Protestants too. But his feelings and policy were hostile to Mary, for she was a Catholic. Mary was sometimes treated very harshly by him, and she was subjected to many privations and hardships on account of her religious faith. The government of Edward justified these measures, on account of the necessity of promoting the Reformation, and discouraging popery by every means in their power. Northumberland supposed, too, that it was safe to do this, for Edward being very young, it was probable that he would live and reign a long time. It is true that Mary was named, in her father's will, as his successor, if she outlived him, but then it was highly probable that she would not outlive him, for she was several years older than he.

All these calculations, however, were spoiled by the sudden failure of Edward's health when he was sixteen years old. Northumberland was much alarmed at this. He knew at once that if Edward should die, and Mary succeed him, all his power would be gone, and he determined to make desperate efforts to prevent such a result.

It must not be understood, however, that in coming to this resolution, Northumberland considered himself as intending and planning a deliberate usurpation of power. There was a real uncertainty in respect to the question who was the true and rightful heir to the crown. Northumberland was, undoubtedly, strongly biased by his interest, but he may have been unconscious of the bias, and in advocating the mode of succession on which the continuance of his own power depended, he may have really believed that he was only maintaining what was in itself rightful and just.

In fact, there is no mode which human ingenuity has ever yet devised for determining the hands in which the supreme executive of a nation shall be lodged, which will always avoid doubt and contention. If this power devolves by hereditary descent, no rules can be made so minute and full as that cases will not sometimes occur that will transcend them. If, on the other hand, the plan of election be adopted, there will often be technical doubts about a portion of the votes, and cases will sometimes occur where the result will depend upon this doubtful portion. Thus there will be disputes under any system, and ambitious men will seize such occasions to struggle for power.

In order that our readers may clearly understand the nature of the plan which Northumberland adopted, we present, on the following page, a sort of genealogical table of the royal family of England in the days of Elizabeth.

TABLE OF THE ROYAL FAMILY OF ENGLAND IN THE TIME OF ELIZABETH.

_____ = 2. KING HENRY VIII. Catharine of Aragon. = 4. QUEEN MARY. Anne Boleyn. = 5. QUEEN ELIZABETH. Jane Seymour. = 3. KING EDWARD VI. Anne of Cleves. Catharine Howard. Catharine Parr.

= Margaret James IV. of Scotland = James V. of Scotland = Mary Queen of Scots 1. KING HENRY VII. = 6. KING JAMES VI. OF SCOTLAND AND I. OF ENGLAND. Earl Of Angus = Margaret Douglas = Earl of Lenox = Lord Darnley

= Mary. Charles Brandon, duke = Frances, marchioness of Suffolk of Dorset = Lady Jane Grey. = Eleanor.

_____

EXPLANATION.

This table gives the immediate descendants of Henry VII., a descent being denoted by the sign =. The names of the persons whom they respectively married are in italics. Those who became sovereigns of England are in small capitals, and the order in which they reigned is denoted by the figures prefixed to their names.

By examination of this table it will be seen that King Henry VII. left a son and two daughters. The son was King Henry VIII., and he had three children. His third child was King Edward VI., who was now about to die. The other two were the Princesses Mary and Elizabeth, who would naturally be considered the next heirs after Edward; and besides, King Henry had left a will, as has been already explained, confirming their rights to the succession. This will he had made near the time of his death; but it will be recollected that, during his life-time, both the marriages from which these princesses had sprung had been formally annulled. His marriage with Catharine of Aragon had been annulled on one plea, and that of Anne Boleyn on another. Both these decrees of annulment had afterward been revoked, and the right of the princesses to succeed had been restored, or attempted to be restored, by the will. Still, it admitted of a question, after all, whether Mary and Elizabeth were to be considered as the children of true and lawful wives or not.

If they were not, then Lady Jane Grey was the next heir, for she was placed next to the princesses by King Henry the Eighth's will. This will, for some reason or other, set aside a the descendants of Margaret, who went to Scotland as the wife of James IV. of that country. What right the king had thus to disinherit the children of his sister Margaret was a great question. Among her descendants was Mary Queen of Scots, as will be seen by the table, and she was, at this time, the representative of that branch of the family. The friends of Mary Queen of Scots claimed that she was the lawful heir to the English throne after Edward. They maintained that the marriage of Catharine, the Princess Mary's mother, and also that of Anne Boleyn, Elizabeth's mother, had both been annulled, and that the will could not restore them. They maintained, also, that the will was equally powerless in setting aside the claims of Margaret, her grandmother. Mary Queen of Scots, though silent now, advanced her claim subsequently, and made Elizabeth a great deal of trouble.

Then there was, besides these, a third party, who maintained that King Henry the Eighth's will was not effectual in legalizing again the annulled marriages, but that it was sufficient to set aside the claims of Margaret. Of course, with them, Lady Jane Grey, who, as will be seen by the table, was the representative of the second sister of Henry VIII., was the only heir. The Earl of Northumberland embraced this view. His motive was to raise Lady Jane Grey to the throne, in order to exclude the Princess Mary, whose accession he knew very well would bring all his greatness to a very sudden end.

The Earl of Northumberland was at this time the principal minister of the young king. The protector Somerset had fallen long ago. Northumberland, whose name was then John Dudley, had supplanted him, and had acquired so great influence and power at court that almost every thing seemed to be at his disposal. He was, however, generally hated by the other courtiers and by the nation. Men who gain the confidence of a young or feeble-minded prince, so as to wield a great power not properly their own, are almost always odious. It was expected, however, that his career would be soon brought to an end, as all knew that King Edward must die, and it was generally understood that Mary was to succeed him.

Northumberland, however, was very anxious to devise some scheme to continue his power, and in revolving the subject in his mind, he conceived of plans which seemed to promise not only to continue, but also greatly to increase it. His scheme was to have the princesses' claims set aside, and Lady Jane Grey raised to the throne. He had several sons. One of them was young, handsome, and accomplished. He thought of proposing him to Lady Jane's father as the husband of Lady Jane, and, to induce the marquis to consent to this plan, he promised to obtain a dukedom for him by means of his influence with the king. The marquis agreed to the proposal. Lady Jane did not object to the husband they offered her. The dukedom was obtained, and the marriage, together with two others which Northumberland had arranged to strengthen his influence, were celebrated, all on the same day, with great festivities and rejoicings. The people looked on moodily, jealous and displeased, though they had no open ground of displeasure, except that it was unsuitable to have such scenes of gayety and rejoicing among the high officers of the court while the young monarch himself was lying upon his dying bed. They did not yet know that it was Northumberland's plan to raise his new daughter-in-law to the throne.

Northumberland thought it would greatly increase his prospect of success if he could obtain some act of acknowledgment of Lady Jane's claims to the crown before Edward died. An opportunity soon occurred for effecting this purpose. One day, as he was sitting by young Edward's bedside, he turned the conversation to the subject of the Reformation, which had made great progress during Edward's reign, and he led Edward on in the conversation, until he remarked that it was a great pity to have the work all undone by Mary's accession, for she was a Catholic, and would, of course, endeavor to bring the country back again under the spiritual dominion of Rome. Northumberland then told him that there was one way, and one way only, to avert such a calamity, and that was to make Lady Jane his heir instead of Mary.

King Edward was a very thoughtful, considerate, and conscientious boy, and was very desirous of doing what he considered his duty. He thought it was his duty to do all in his power to sustain the Reformation, and to prevent the Catholic power from gaining ascendency in England again. He was, therefore, easily persuaded to accede to Northumberland's plan, especially as he was himself strongly attached to Lady Jane, who had often been his playmate and companion.

The king accordingly sent for three judges of the realm, and directed them to draw up a deed of assignment, by which the crown was to be conveyed to Lady Jane on the young king's death, Mary and Elizabeth being alike excluded. The judges were afraid to do this; for, by King Henry the Eighth's settlement of the crown, all those persons who should do any thing to disturb the succession as he arranged it were declared to be guilty of high treason. The judges knew very well, therefore, that if they should do what the king required of them, and then, if the friends of Lady Jane should fail of establishing her upon the throne, the end of the affair would be the cutting off of their own heads in the Tower. They represented this to the king, and begged to be excused from the duty that he required of them. Northumberland was in a great rage at this, and seemed almost ready to break out against the judges in open violence. They, however, persisted in their refusal to do what they well knew would subject them to the pains and penalties of treason.

Northumberland, finding that threats and violence would not succeed, contrived another mode of obviating the difficulty. He proposed to protect the judges from any possible evil consequences of their act by a formal pardon for it, signed by the king, and sealed with the great seal, so that, in case they were ever charged with treason, the pardon would save them from punishment. This plan succeeded. The pardon was made out, being written with great formality upon a parchment roll, and sealed with the great seal. The judges then prepared and signed the deed of settlement by which the crown was given to Lady Jane, though, after all, they did it with much reluctance and many forebodings.

Northumberland next wanted to contrive some plan for getting the princesses into his power, in order to prevent their heading any movement in behalf of their own claims at the death of the king. He was also desirous of making such arrangements as to conceal the death of the king for a few days after it should take place, in order that he might get Lady Jane and her officers in complete possession of the kingdom before the demise of the crown should be generally known. For this purpose he dismissed the regular physicians who had attended upon the king, and put him under the charge of a woman, who pretended that she had a medicine that would certainly cure him. He sent, also, messengers to the princesses, who were then in the country north of London, requesting that they would come to Greenwich, to be near the sick chamber where their brother was lying, that they might cheer and comfort him in his sickness and pain.

The princesses obeyed the summons. They each set out immediately on the journey, and moved toward London on their way to Greenwich. In the mean time, Edward was rapidly declining. The change in the treatment which took place when his physicians left him, made him worse instead of better. His cough increased, his breathing became more labored and difficult; in a word, his case presented all the symptoms of approaching dissolution. At length he died. Northumberland attempted to keep the fact concealed until after the princesses should arrive, that he might get them into his power. Some faithful friend, however, made all haste to meet them, in order to inform them what was going on. In this way Mary received intelligence of her brother's death when she had almost reached London, and was informed, also, of the plans of Northumberland for raising Lady Jane to the throne. The two princesses were extremely alarmed, and both turned back at once toward the northward again. Mary stopped to write a letter to the council, remonstrating against their delay in proclaiming her queen, and then proceeded rapidly to a strong castle at a place called Framlingham, in the county of Suffolk, on the eastern coast of England. She made this her head-quarters, because she supposed that the people of that county were particularly friendly to her; and then, besides, it was near the sea, and, in case the course of events should turn against her, she could make her escape to foreign lands. It is true that the prospect of being fugitive and an exile was very dark and gloomy, but it was not so terrible as the idea of being shut up a prisoner in the Tower, or being beheaded on a block for treason.

In the mean time, Northumberland went, at the head of a troop of his adherents, to the residence of Lady Jane Grey, informed her of the death of Edward, and announced to her their determination to proclaim her queen. Lady Jane was very much astonished at this news. At first she absolutely refused the offered honor; but the solicitations and urgency of Northumberland, and of her father and her young husband, at length prevailed. She was conducted to London, and instated in at least the semblance of power.

As the news of these transactions spread throughout the land, a universal and strong excitement was produced, every body at once taking sides either for Mary or Lady Jane. Bands of armed men began to assemble. It soon became apparent, however, that, beyond the immediate precincts of London, the country was almost unanimous for Mary. They dreaded, it is true, the danger which they anticipated from her Catholic faith, but still they had all considered it a settled point, since the death of Henry the Eighth, that Mary was to reign whenever Edward should die; and this general expectation that she would be queen had passed insensibly into an opinion that she ought to be. Considered strictly as a legal question, it was certainly doubtful which of the four claimants to the throne had the strongest title; but the public were not disposed so to regard it. They chose, on the whole, that Mary should reign. Large military masses consequently flocked to her standard. Elizabeth took sides with her, and, as it was important to give as much public effect to her adhesion as possible, they furnished Elizabeth with a troop of a thousand horsemen, at the head of which she rode to meet Mary and tender her aid.

Northumberland went forth at the head of such forces as he could collect, but he soon found that the attempt was vain. His troops forsook him. The castles which had at first been under his command surrendered themselves to Mary. The Tower of London went over to her side. Finally, all being lost, Northumberland himself was taken prisoner, and all his influential friends with him, and were committed to the Tower. Lady Jane herself too, together with her husband and father, were seized and sent to prison.

Northumberland was immediately put upon his trial for treason. He was condemned, and brought at once to the block. In fact, the whole affair moved very promptly and rapidly on, from its commencement to its consummation. Edward the Sixth died on the 5th of July, and it was only the 22d of August when Northumberland was beheaded. The period for which the unhappy Lady Jane enjoyed the honor of being called a queen was nine days.

It was about a month after this that Mary passed from the Tower through the city of London in a grand triumphal procession to be crowned. The royal chariot, covered with cloth of golden tissue, was drawn by six horses most splendidly caparisoned. Elizabeth, who had aided her sister, so far as she could, in the struggle, was admitted to share the triumph. She had a carriage drawn by six horses too, with cloth and decorations of silver. They proceeded in this manner, attended and followed by a great cavalcade of nobles and soldiery, to

Westminster Abbey, where Mary took her seat with great formality upon her father's throne.

CHAPTER IV.

THE SPANISH MATCH.

1553-1555

Queen Mary's character.--Bigotry and firmness.--Suitors for Queen Mary's hand.--Emperor Charles the Fifth.--Character of his son Philip.--The emperor proposes his son.--Mary pleased with the proposal.--Plans of the ministers.--The people alarmed.--Opposition to the match.--The emperor furnishes money.--The emperor's embassy.--Stipulations of the treaty of marriage.--Wyatt's rebellion.--Duke of Suffolk.--Wyatt advances toward London.--The queen retreats into the city.--Wyatt surrenders.--The Duke of Suffolk sent to the Tower.--Beheading of Lady Jane Grey.--Her heroic fortitude.--Death of Suffolk.--Imprisonment of Elizabeth.--Execution of Wyatt.--The wedding plan proceeds.--Hostility of the sailors.--Mary's fears and complainings.--Philip lands at Southampton.--Philip's proud and haughty demeanor.--The marriage ceremony.--Philip abandons Mary.--Her repinings.--Her death.

When Queen Mary ascended the throne, she was a maiden lady not far from thirty-five years of age. She was cold, austere, and forbidding in her appearance and manners, though probably conscientious and honest in her convictions of duty. She was a very firm and decided Catholic, or, rather, she evinced a certain strict adherence to the principles of her religious faith, which we generally call firmness when it is exhibited by those whose opinions agree with our own, though we are very apt to name it bigotry in those who differ from us.

For instance, when the body of young Edward, her brother, after his death, was to be deposited in the last home of the English kings in Westminster Abbey, which is a very magnificent cathedral a little way up the river from

London, the services were, of course, conducted according to the ritual of the English Church, which was then Protestant. Mary, however, could not conscientiously countenance such services even by being present at them. She accordingly assembled her immediate attendants and personal friends in her own private chapel, and celebrated the interment there, with Catholic priests, by a service conformed to the Catholic ritual. Was it a bigoted, or only a firm and proper, attachment to her own faith, which forbade her joining in the national commemoration? The reader must decide; but, in deciding, he is bound to render the same verdict that he would have given if it had been a case of a Protestant withdrawing thus from Catholic forms.

At all events, whether bigoted or not, Mary was doubtless sincere; but she was so cold, and stern, and austere in her character, that she was very little likely to be loved. There were a great many persons who wished to become her husband, but their motives were to share her grandeur and power. Among these persons, the most prominent one, and the one apparently most likely to succeed, was a prince of Spain. His name was Philip.

[Illustration: PORTRAIT OF PHILIP OF SPAIN.]

It was his father's plan, and not his own, that he should marry Queen Mary. His father was at this time the most wealthy and powerful monarch in Europe. His name was Charles. He is commonly called in history Charles V. of Spain. He was not only King of Spain, but Emperor of Germany. He resided sometimes at Madrid, and sometimes at Brussels in Flanders. His son Philip had been married to a Portuguese princess, but his wife had died, and thus Philip was a widower. Still, he was only twenty-seven years of age, but he was as stern, severe, and repulsive in his manners as Mary. His personal appearance, too, corresponded with his character. He was a very decided Catholic also, and in his natural spirit, haughty, ambitious, and domineering.

The Emperor Charles, as soon as he heard of young Edward's death and of Mary's accession to the English throne, conceived the plan of proposing to her his son Philip for a husband. He sent over a wise and sagacious statesman from his court to make the proposition, and to urge it by such reasons as would be most likely to influence Mary's mind, and the minds of the great officers of her government. The embassador managed the affair well. In fact, it was probably easy to manage it. Mary would naturally be pleased with the idea of such a young husband, who, besides being young and accomplished, was the son of the greatest potentate in Europe, and likely one day to take his father's place in that lofty elevation. Besides, Mary Queen of Scots, who had rival claims to Queen Mary's throne, had married, or was about to marry, the son of the King of France, and there was a little glory in outshining her, by having for a husband a son of the King of Spain. It might, however, perhaps, be a question which was the greatest match; for, though the court of Paris was the most brilliant, Spain, being at that time possessed of the gold and silver mines of its American colonies, was at least the richestcountry in the world.

Mary's ministers, when they found that Mary herself liked the plan, fell in with it too. Mary had been beginning, very quietly indeed, but very efficiently, her measures for bringing back the English government and nation to the Catholic faith. Her ministers told her now, however, that if she wished to succeed in effecting this match, she must suspend all these plans until the match was consummated. The people of England were generally of the Protestant faith. They had been very uneasy and restless under the progress which the queen had been making in silencing Protestant preachers, and bringing back Catholic rites and ceremonies; and now, if they found that their queen was going to marry so rigid and uncompromising a Catholic as Philip of Spain, they would be doubly alarmed. She must suspend, therefore, for a time, her measures for restoring papacy, unless she was willing to give up her husband. The queen saw that this was the alternative, and she decided on following her ministers' advice. She did all in her power to quiet and calm the public mind, in order to prepare the way for announcing the proposed connection.

Rumors, however, began to be spread abroad that such a design was entertained before Mary was fully prepared to promulgate it. These rumors produced great excitement, and awakened strong opposition. The people knew

Philip's ambitious and overbearing character, and they believed that if he were to come to England as the husband of the queen, the whole government would pass into his hands, and, as he would naturally be very much under the influence of his father, the connection was likely to result in making England a mere appendage to the already vast dominions of the emperor. The House of Commons appointed a committee of twenty members, and sent them to the queen, with a humble petition that she would not marry a foreigner. The queen was much displeased at receiving such a petition, and she dissolved the Parliament. The members dispersed, carrying with them every where expressions of their dissatisfaction and fear. England, they said, was about to become a province of Spain, and the prospect of such a consummation, wherever the tidings went, filled the people of the country with great alarm.

Queen Mary's principal minister of state at this time was a crafty politician, whose name was Gardiner. Gardiner sent word to the emperor that there was great opposition to his son's marriage in England, and that he feared that he should not be able to accomplish it, unless the terms of the contract of marriage were made very favorable to the queen and to England, and unless the emperor could furnish him with a large sum of money to use as a means of bringing influential persons of the realm to favor it. Charles decided to send the money. He borrowed it of some of the rich cities of Germany, making his son Philip give his bond to repay it as soon as he should get possession of his bride, and of the rich and powerful country over which she reigned. The amount thus remitted to England is said by the historians of those days to have been a sum equal to two millions of dollars. The bribery was certainly on a very respectable scale.

The emperor also sent a very magnificent embassy to London, with a distinguished nobleman at its head, to arrange the terms and contracts of the marriage. This embassy came in great state, and, during their residence in London, were the objects of great attention and parade. The eclat of their reception, and the influence of the bribes, seemed to silence opposition to the scheme. Open opposition ceased to be expressed, though a strong and inveterate determination against the measure was secretly extending itself throughout the realm. This, however, did not prevent the negotiations from going on. The terms were probably all fully understood and agreed upon before the embassy came, so that nothing remained but the formalities of writing and signing the articles.

Some of the principal stipulations of these articles were, that Philip was to have the title of King of England jointly with Mary's title of queen. Mary was also to share with him, in the same way, his titles in Spain. It was agreed that Mary should have the exclusive power of the appointment of officers of government in England, and that no Spaniards should be eligible at all. Particular provisions were made in respect to the children which might result from the marriage, as to how they should inherit rights of government in the two countries. Philip had one son already, by his former wife. This son was to succeed his father in the kingdom of Spain, but the other dominions of Philip on the Continent were to descend to the offspring of this new marriage, in modes minutely specified to fit all possible cases which might occur. The making of all these specifications, however, turned out to be labor lost, as Mary never had children.

It was also specially agreed that Philip should not bring Spanish or foreign domestics into the realm, to give uneasiness to the English people; that he would never take the queen out of England, nor carry any of the children away, without the consent of the English nobility; and that, if the queen were to die before him, all his rights and claims of every sort, in respect to England, should forever cease. He also agreed that he would never carry away any of the jewels or other property of the crown, nor suffer any other person to do so.

These stipulations, guarding so carefully the rights of Mary and of England, were intended to satisfy the English people, and remove their objections to the match. They produced some effect, but the hostility was too deeply seated to be so easily allayed. It grew, on the contrary, more and more threatening, until at length a conspiracy was formed by a number of influential and powerful men, and a plan of open rebellion organized.

The leader in this plan was Sir Thomas Wyatt, and the outbreak which followed is known in history as Wyatt's rebellion. Another of the leaders was the Duke of Suffolk, who, it will be recollected, was the father of Lady Jane Grey. This led people to suppose that the plan of the conspirators was not merely to prevent the consummation of the Spanish match, but to depose Queen Mary entirely, and to raise the Lady Jane to the throne. However this may be, an extensive and formidable conspiracy was formed. There were to have been several risings in different parts of the kingdom. They all failed except the one which Wyatt himself was to head, which was in Kent, in the southeastern part of the country. This succeeded so far, at least, that a considerable force was collected, and began to advance toward London from the southern side.

Queen Mary was very much alarmed. She had no armed force in readiness to encounter this danger. She sent messengers across the Thames and down the river to meet Wyatt, who was advancing at the head of four thousand men, to ask what it was that he demanded. He replied that the queen must be delivered up as his prisoner, and also the Tower of London be surrendered to him. This showed that his plan was to depose the queen. Mary rejected these proposals at once, and, having no forces to meet this new enemy, she had to retreat from Westminster into the city of London, and here she took refuge in the city hall, called the Guildhall, and put herself under the protection of the city authorities. Some of her friends urged her to take shelter in the Tower; but she had more confidence, she said, in the faithfulness and loyalty of her subjects than in castle walls.

Wyatt continued to advance. He was still upon the south side of the river. There was but one bridge across the Thames, at London, in those days, though there are half a dozen now, and this one was so strongly barricaded and guarded that Wyatt did not dare to attempt to cross it. He went up the river, therefore, to cross at a higher point; and this circuit, and several accidental circumstances which occurred, detained him so long that a considerable force had been got together to receive him when he was ready to enter the city. He pushed boldly on into the narrow streets, which received him like a trap or a snare. The city troops hemmed up his way after he had entered. They barricaded the streets, they shut the gates, and armed men poured in to take possession of all the avenues. Wyatt depended upon finding the people of London on his side. They turned, instead, against him. All hope of success in his enterprise, and all possibility of escape from his own awful danger, disappeared together. A herald came from the queen's officer calling upon him to surrender himself quietly, and save the effusion of blood. He surrendered in an agony of terror and despair.

The Duke of Suffolk learned these facts in another county, where he was endeavoring to raise a force to aid Wyatt. He immediately fled, and hid himself in the house of one of his domestics. He was betrayed, however, seized, and sent to the Tower. Many other prominent actors in the insurrection were arrested, and the others fled in all directions, wherever they could find concealment or safety.

Lady Jane's life had been spared thus far, although she had been, in fact, guilty of treason against Mary by the former attempt to take the crown. She now, however, two days after the capture of Wyatt, received word that she must prepare to die. She was, of course, surprised and shocked at the suddenness of this announcement; but she soon regained her composure, and passed through the awful scenes preceding her death with a fortitude amounting to heroism, which was very astonishing in one so young. Her husband was to die too. He was beheaded first, and she saw the headless body, as it was brought back from the place of execution, before her turn came. She acknowledged her guilt in having attempted to seize her cousin's crown. As the attempt to seize this crown failed, mankind consider her technically guilty. If it had succeeded, Mary, instead of Jane, would have been the traitor who would have died for attempting criminally to usurp a throne.

In the mean time Wyatt and Suffolk remained prisoners in the Tower. Suffolk was overwhelmed with remorse and sorrow at having been the means, by his selfish ambition, of the cruel death of so innocent and lovely a child. He did not suffer this anguish long, however, for five days after his son and Lady Jane were executed, his head fell too from the block. Wyatt was reserved a little longer.

He was more formally tried, and in his examination he asserted that the Princess Elizabeth was involved in the conspiracy. Officers were immediately sent to arrest Elizabeth. She was taken to a royal palace at Westminster, just above London, called Whitehall, and shut up there in close confinement, and no one was allowed to visit her or speak to her. The particulars of this imprisonment will be described more fully in the next chapter. Fifty or sixty common conspirators, not worthy of being beheaded with an ax, were hanged, and a company of six hundred more were brought, their hands tied, and halters about their necks, a miserable gang, into Mary's presence, before her palace, to be pardoned. Wyatt was then executed. When he came to die, however, he retracted what he had alleged of Elizabeth. He declared that she was entirely innocent of any participation in the scheme of rebellion. Elizabeth's friends believe that he accused her because he supposed that such a charge would be agreeable to Mary, and that he should himself be more leniently treated in consequence of it, but that when at last he found that sacrificing her would not save him, his guilty conscience scourged him into doing her justice in his last hours.

All obstacles to the wedding were now apparently removed; for, after the failure of Wyatt's rebellion, nobody dared to make any open opposition to the plans of the queen, though there was still abundance of secret dissatisfaction. Mary was now very impatient to have the marriage carried into effect. A new Parliament was called, and its concurrence in the plan obtained. Mary ordered a squadron of ships to be fitted out and sent to Spain, to convey the bridegroom to England. The admiral who had command of this fleet wrote to her that the sailors were so hostile to Philip that he did not think it was safe for her to intrust him to their hands. Mary then commanded this force to be dismissed, in order to arrange some other way to bring Philip over. She was then full of anxiety and apprehension lest some accident might befall him. His ship might be wrecked, or he might fall into the hands of the French, who were not at all well disposed toward the match. Her thoughts and her conversation were running upon this topic all the time. She was restless by day and sleepless by night, until her health was at last seriously impaired, and her friends began really to fear that she might lose her reason. She was very anxious, too, lest Philip should find her beauty so impaired by her years, and by the state of her health, that she should fail, when he arrived, of becoming the object of his love.

In fact, she complained already that Philip neglected her. He did not write to her, or express in any way the interest and affection which she thought ought to be awakened in his mind by a bride who, as she expressed it, was going to bring a kingdom for a dowry. This sort of cold and haughty demeanor was, however, in keeping with the self-importance and the pride which then often marked the Spanish character, and which, in Philip particularly, always seemed to be extreme.

At length the time arrived for his embarkation. He sailed across the Bay of Biscay, and up the English Channel until he reached Southampton, a famous port on the southern coast of England. There he landed with great pomp and parade. He assumed a very proud and stately bearing, which made a very unfavorable impression upon the English people who had been sent by Queen Mary to receive him. He drew his sword when he landed, and walked about with it, for a time, in a very pompous manner, holding the sword unsheathed in his hand, the crowd of by-standers that had collected to witness the spectacle of the landing looking on all the time, and wondering what such an action could be intended to intimate. It was probably intended simply to make them wonder. The authorities of Southampton had arranged it to come in procession to meet Philip, and present him with the keys of the gates, an emblem of an honorable reception into the city. Philip received the keys, but did not deign a word of reply. The distance and reserve which it had been customary to maintain between the English sovereigns and their people was always pretty strongly marked, but Philip's loftiness and grandeur seemed to surpass all bounds.

Mary went two thirds of the way from London to the coast to meet the bridegroom. Here the marriage ceremony was performed, and the whole party came, with great parade and rejoicings, back to London, and Mary, satisfied and happy, took up her abode with her new lord in Windsor Castle.

The poor queen was, however, in the end, sadly disappointed in her husband. He felt no love for her; he was probably, in fact, incapable of love. He remained in England a year, and then, growing weary of his wife and of his adopted country, he went back to Spain again, greatly to Queen Mary's vexation and chagrin. They were both extremely disappointed in not having children. Philip's motive for marrying Mary was ambition wholly, and not love; and when he found that an heir to inherit the two kingdoms was not to be expected, he treated his unhappy wife with great neglect and cruelty and finally went away from her altogether. He came back again, it is true, a year afterward, but it was only to compel Mary to join with him in a war against France. He told her that if she would not do this, he would go away from England and never see her again. Mary yielded; but at length, harassed and worn down with useless regrets and repinings, her mental sufferings are supposed to have shortened her days. She died miserably a few years after her marriage, and thus the Spanish match turned out to be a very unfortunate match indeed.

CHAPTER V.

ELIZABETH IN THE TOWER.

1554-1555

Elizabeth's position.--Legitimacy of Mary and Elizabeth's birth.--Mary and Elizabeth's differences.--Courteney's long imprisonment.--Mary's attentions to Courteney.--Courteney's attentions to Elizabeth.--Mary's plan to get Elizabeth in her power.--Elizabeth's wariness.--Wyatt accuses Elizabeth.--Her seizure.-- Elizabeth borne in a litter.--She is examined and released.--Elizabeth again arrested.--Her letter to Mary.--Situation of the Tower.--The Traitors' Gate.-- Elizabeth conveyed to the Tower.--She is landed at the Traitors' Gate.--

Elizabeth's reception at the Tower.--Her unwillingness to enter.--Elizabeth's indignation and grief.--She is closely imprisoned.--Elizabeth in the garden.--The little child and the flowers.--Elizabeth greatly alarmed.--Her removal from the Tower.--Elizabeth's fears.--Mary's designs.--Elizabeth taken to Richmond.--Mary's plan for marrying her.--Elizabeth's journey to Woodstock.--Christmas festivities.--Elizabeth persists in her innocence.--The torch-light visit.--Reconciliation between Elizabeth and Mary.--Elizabeth's release.

The imprisonment of Queen Elizabeth in the Tower, which was briefly alluded to in the last chapter, deserves a more full narration than was possible to give to it there. She had retired from court some time before the difficulties about the Spanish match arose. It is true that she took sides with Mary in the contest with Northumberland and the friends of Jane Grey, and she shared her royal sister's triumph in the pomp and parade of the coronation; but, after all, she and Mary could not possibly be very good friends. The marriages of their respective mothers could not both have been valid. Henry the Eighth was so impatient that he could not wait for a divorce from Catharine before he married Anne Boleyn. The only way to make the latter marriage legal, therefore, was to consider the former one null and void from the beginning, and if the former one was not thus null and void, the latter must be so. If Henry had waited for a divorce, then both marriages might have been valid, each for the time of its own continuance, and both the princesses might have been lawful heirs; but as it was, neither of them could maintain her own claims to be considered a lawful daughter, without denying, by implication at least, those of the other. They were therefore, as it were, natural enemies. Though they might be outwardly civil to each other, it was not possible that there could be any true harmony or friendship between them.

A circumstance occurred, too, soon after Mary's accession to the throne, which resulted in openly alienating the feelings of the two ladies from each other. There was a certain prisoner in the Tower of London, a gentleman of high rank and great consideration, named Courteney, now about twenty-six years of age, who had been imprisoned in the Tower by King Henry the Eighth when he was only twelve years old, on account of some political offenses of his father! He had thus been a close prisoner for fourteen years at Mary's accession; but Mary released him. It was found, when he returned to society again, that he had employed his solitary hours in cultivating his mind, acquiring knowledge, and availing himself of all the opportunities for improvement which his situation afforded, and that he came forth an intelligent, accomplished, and very agreeable man. The interest which his appearance and manners excited was increased by the sympathy naturally felt for the sufferings that he had endured. In a word, he became a general favorite. The rank of his family was high enough for Mary to think of him for her husband, for this was before the Spanish match was thought of. Mary granted him a title, and large estates, and showed him many other favors, and, as every body supposed, tried very hard to make an impression on his heart. Her efforts were, however, vain. Courteney gave an obvious preference to Elizabeth, who was young then, at least, if not beautiful. This successful rivalry on the part of her sister filled the queen's heart with resentment and envy, and she exhibited her chagrin by so many little marks of neglect and incivility, that Elizabeth's resentment was roused in its turn, and she asked permission to retire from court to her residence in the country. Mary readily gave the permission, and thus it happened that when Wyatt's rebellion first broke out, as described in the last chapter, Elizabeth was living in retirement and seclusion at Ashridge, an estate of hers at some distance west of London. As to Courteney, Mary found some pretext or other for sending him back again to his prison in the Tower.

Mary was immediately afraid that the malcontents would join with Elizabeth and attempt to put forward her name and her claims to the crown, which, if they were to do, it would make their movement very formidable. She was impressed immediately with the idea that it was of great importance to get Elizabeth back again into her power. The most probable way of succeeding in doing this, she thought, was to write her a kind and friendly letter, inviting her to return. She accordingly wrote such a letter. She said in it that certain evil-disposed persons were plotting some disturbances in the kingdom, and that she thought that Elizabeth was not safe where she was. She urged her, therefore, to return, saying that she should be truly welcome, and should be protected against all danger if she would come.

An invitation from a queen is a command, and Elizabeth would have felt bound to obey this summons, but she was sick when it came. At least she was not well, and she was not much disposed to underrate her sickness for the sake of being able to travel on this occasion. The officers of her household made out a formal certificate to the effect that Elizabeth was not able to undertake such a journey.

In the mean time Wyatt's rebellion broke out; he marched to London, was entrapped there and taken prisoner, as is related at length in the last chapter. In his confessions he implicated the Princess Elizabeth, and also Courteney, and Mary's government then determined that they must secure Elizabeth's person at all events, sick or well. They sent, therefore, three gentlemen as commissioners, with a troop of horse to attend them, to bring her to London. They carried the queen's litter with them, to bring the princess upon it in case she should be found unable to travel in any other way.

This party arrived at Ashridge at ten o'clock at night. They insisted on being admitted at once into the chamber of Elizabeth, and there they made known their errand. Elizabeth was terrified; she begged not to be moved, as she was really too sick to go. They called in some physicians, who certified that she could be moved without danger to her life. The next morning they put her upon the litter, a sort of covered bed, formed like a palanquin, and borne, like a palanquin, by men. It was twenty-nine miles to London, and it took the party four days to reach the city, they moved so slowly. This circumstance is mentioned sometimes as showing how sick Elizabeth must have been. But the fact is, there was no reason whatever for any haste. Elizabeth was now completely in Mary's power, and it could make no possible difference how long she was upon the road.

The litter passed along the roads in great state. It was a princess that they were bearing. As they approached London, a hundred men in handsome uniforms went before, and an equal number followed. A great many people came out from the city to meet the princess, as a token of respect. This displeased Mary, but it could not well be prevented or punished. On their arrival they took Elizabeth to one of the palaces at Westminster, called Whitehall. She was examined by Mary's privy council. Nothing was proved against her, and, as the rebellion seemed now wholly at an end, she was at length released, and thus ended her first durance as a political prisoner.

It happened, however, that other persons implicated in Wyatt's plot, when examined, made charges against Elizabeth in respect to it, and Queen Mary sent another force and arrested her again. She was taken now to a famous royal palace, called Hampton Court, which is situated on the Thames, a few miles above the city. She brought many of the officers of her household and of her personal attendants with her; but one of the queen's ministers, accompanied by two other officers, came soon after, and dismissed all her own attendants, and placed persons in the service of the queen in their place. They also set a guard around the palace, and then left the princess, for the night, a close prisoner, and yet without any visible signs of coercion, for all these guards might be guards of honor.

The next day some officers came again, and told her that it had been decided to send her to the Tower, and that a barge was ready at the river to convey her. She was very much agitated and alarmed, and begged to be allowed to send a letter to her sister before they took her away. One of the officers insisted that she should have the privilege, and the other that she should not. The former conquered in the contest, and Elizabeth wrote the letter and sent it. It contained an earnest and solemn disavowal of all participation in the plots which she had been charged with encouraging, and begged Mary to believe that she was innocent, and allow her to be released.

The letter did no good. Elizabeth was taken into the barge and conveyed in a very private manner down the river. Hampton Court is above London, several miles, and the Tower is just below the city. There are several entrances to this vast castle, some of them by stairs from the river. Among these is one by which prisoners accused of great political crimes were usually taken in, and which is called the Traitors' Gate. There was another entrance, also, from the river, by which a more honorable admission to the fortress might be attained. The Tower was not solely a prison. It was often a place of retreat for kings and queens from any sudden danger, and was frequently occupied by them as a somewhat permanent residence. There were a great number of structures within the walls, in some of which royal apartments were fitted up with great splendor. Elizabeth had often been in the Tower as a resident or a visitor, and thus far there was nothing in the circumstances of the case to forbid the supposition that they might be taking her there as a guest or resident now. She was anxious and uneasy, it is true, but she was not certain that she was regarded as a prisoner.

In the mean time, the barge, with the other boats in attendance, passed down the river in the rain, for it was a stormy day, a circumstance which aided the authorities in their effort to convey their captive to her gloomy prison without attracting the attention of the populace. Besides, it was the day of some great religious festival, when the people were generally in the churches. This day had been chosen on that very account. The barge and the boats came down the river, therefore, without attracting much attention; they approached the landing-place at last, and stopped at the flight of steps leading up from the water to the Traitors' Gate.

Elizabeth declared that she was no traitor, and that she would not be landed there. The nobleman who had charge of her told her simply, in reply, that she could not have her choice of a place to land. At the same time, he offered her his cloak to protect her from the rain in passing from the barge to the castle gate. Umbrellas had not been invented in those days. Elizabeth threw the cloak away from her in vexation and anger. She found, however, that it was of no use to resist. She could not choose. She stepped from the barge out upon the stairs in the rain, saying, as she did so, "Here lands as true and faithful a subject as ever landed a prisoner at these stairs. Before thee, O God, I speak it, having now no friends but thee alone."

A large company of the warders and keepers of the castle had been drawn up at the Traitors' Gate to receive her, as was customary on occasions when prisoners of high rank were to enter the Tower. As these men were always dressed in uniform of a peculiar antique character, such a parade of them made quite an imposing appearance. Elizabeth asked what it meant. They told her that that was the customary mode of receiving a prisoner. She said that if it was, she hoped that they would dispense with the ceremony in her case, and asked that, for her sake, the men might be dismissed from such attendance in so inclement a season. The men blessed her for her goodness, and kneeled down and prayed that God would preserve her.

She was extremely unwilling to go into the prison. As they approached the part of the edifice where she was to be confined, through the court-yard of the Tower, she stopped and sat down upon a stone, perhaps a step, or the curb stone of a walk. The lieutenant urged her to go in out of the cold and wet. "Better sitting here than in a worse place," she replied, "for God knoweth whither you are bringing me." However, she rose and went on. She entered the prison, was conducted to her room, and the doors were locked and bolted upon her.

Elizabeth was kept closely imprisoned for a month; after that, some little relaxation in the strictness of her seclusion was allowed. Permission was very reluctantly granted to her to walk every day in the royal apartments, which were now unoccupied, so that there was no society to be found there, but it afforded her a sort of pleasure to range through them for recreation and exercise. But this privilege could not be accorded without very strict limitations and conditions. Two officers of the Tower and three women had to attend her; the windows, too, were shut, and she was not permitted to go and look out at them. This was rather melancholy recreation, it must be allowed, but it was better than being shut up all day in a single apartment, bolted and barred.

There was a small garden within the castle not far from the prison, and after some time Elizabeth was permitted to walk there. The gates and doors, however, were kept carefully closed, and all the prisoners, whose rooms looked into it from the surrounding buildings, were closely watched by their respective keepers, while Elizabeth was in the garden, to prevent their having any communication with her by looks or signs. There were a great many persons confined at this time, who had been arrested on charges connected with Wyatt's rebellion, and the authorities seem to have been very specially vigilant to prevent the possibility of Elizabeth's having communication with any of them. There was a little child of five years of age who used to come and visit Elizabeth in her room, and bring her flowers. He was the son of one of the subordinate officers of the Tower. It was, however, at last suspected that he was acting as a messenger between Elizabeth and Courteney. Courteney, it will be recollected, had been sent by Mary back to the Tower again, so that he and Elizabeth were now suffering the same hard fate in neighboring cells. When the boy was suspected of bearing communications between these friends and companions in suffering, he was called before an officer and closely examined. His answers were all open and childlike, and gave no confirmation to the idea which had been entertained. The child, however, was forbidden to go to Elizabeth's apartment any more. He was very much grieved at this, and he watched for the next time that Elizabeth was to walk in the garden, and putting his mouth to a hole in the gate, he called out, "Lady, I can not bring you any more flowers."

After Elizabeth had been thus confined about three months, she was one day terribly alarmed by the sounds of martial parade within the Tower, produced by the entrance of an officer from Queen Mary, named Sir Thomas Beddingfield, at the head of three hundred men. Elizabeth supposed that they were come to execute sentence of death upon her. She asked immediately if the platform on which Lady Jane Grey was beheaded had been taken away. They told her that it had been removed. She was then somewhat relieved. They afterward told her that Sir Thomas had come to take her away from the Tower, but that it was not known where she was to go. This alarmed her again, and she sent for the constable of the Tower, whose name was Lord Chandos, and questioned him very closely to learn what they were going to do with her. He said that it had been decided to remove her from the Tower, and send her to a place called Woodstock, where she was to remain under Sir Thomas Beddingfield's custody, at a royal palace which was situated there. Woodstock is forty or fifty miles to the westward of London, and not far from the city of Oxford.

Elizabeth was very much alarmed at this intelligence. Her mind was filled with vague and uncertain fears and forebodings, which were none the less oppressive for being uncertain and vague. She had, however, no immediate cause for apprehension. Mary found that there was no decisive evidence against her, and did not dare to keep her a prisoner in the Tower too long. There was a large and influential part of the kingdom who were Protestants. They were jealous of the progress Mary was making toward bringing the Catholic religion in again. They abhorred the Spanish match. They naturally looked to Elizabeth as their leader and head, and Mary thought that by too great or too long-continued harshness in her treatment of Elizabeth, she would only exasperate them, and perhaps provoke a new outbreak against her authority. She determined, therefore, to remove the princess from the Tower to some less odious place of confinement.

She was taken first to Queen Mary's court, which was then held at Richmond, just above London; but she was surrounded here by soldiers and guards, and confined almost as strictly as before. She was destined, however, here to another surprise. It was a proposition of marriage. Mary had been arranging a plan for making her the wife of a certain personage styled the Duke of Savoy. His dominions were on the confines of Switzerland and France, and Mary thought that if her rival were once married and removed there, all the troubles which she, Mary, had experienced on her account would be ended forever. She thought, too, that her sister would be glad to accept this offer, which opened such an immediate escape from the embarrassments and sufferings of her situation in England. But Elizabeth was prompt, decided, and firm in the rejection of this plan. England was her home, and to be Queen of England the end and aim of all her wishes and plans. She had rather continue a captive for the present in her native land, than to live in splendor as the consort of a sovereign duke beyond the Rhone.

Mary then ordered Sir Thomas Beddingfield to take her to Woodstock. She traveled on horseback, and was several days on the journey. Her passage through the country attracted great attention. The people assembled by the wayside, expressing their kind wishes, and offering her gifts. The bells were rung in the villages through which she passed. She arrived finally at Woodstock, and was shut up in the palace there.

This was in July, and she remained in Woodstock more than a year, not, however, always very closely confined. At Christmas she was taken to court, and allowed to share in the festivities and rejoicings. On this occasion--it was the first Christmas after the marriage of Mary and Philip--the great hall of the palace was illuminated with a thousand lamps. The princess sat at table next to the king and queen. She was on other occasions, too, taken away for a time, and then returned again to her seclusion at Woodstock. These changes, perhaps, only served to make her feel more than ever the hardships of her lot. They say that one day, as she sat at her window, she heard a milk-maid singing in the fields, in a blithe and merry strain, and said, with a sigh, that she wished she was a milk-maid too.

King Philip, after his marriage, gradually interested himself in her behalf, and exerted his influence to have her released; and Mary's ministers had frequent interviews with her, and endeavored to induce her to make some confession of guilt, and to petition Mary for release as a matter of mercy. They could not, they said, release her while she persisted in her innocence, without admitting that they and Mary had been in the wrong, and had imprisoned her unjustly. But the princess was immovable. She declared that she was perfectly innocent, and that she would never, therefore, say that she was guilty. She would rather remain in prison for the truth, than be at liberty and have it believed that she had been guilty of disloyalty and treason.

At length, one evening in May, Elizabeth received a summons to go to the palace and visit Mary in her chamber. She was conducted there by torch-light. She had a long interview with the queen, the conversation being partly in English and partly in Spanish. It was not very satisfactory on either side. Elizabeth persisted in asserting her innocence, but in other respects she spoke in a kind and conciliatory manner to the queen. The interview ended in a sort of reconciliation. Mary put a valuable ring upon Elizabeth's finger in token of the renewal of friendship, and soon afterward the long period of restraint and confinement was ended, and the princess returned to her own estate at Hatfield in Hertfordshire, where she lived some time in seclusion, devoting herself, in a great measure, to the study of Latin and Greek, under the instructions of Roger Ascham.

CHAPTER VI.

ACCESSION TO THE THRONE

1555-1558

Mary's unhappy reign.--Unrequited love.--Mary's sufferings.--Her religious principles.--Progress of Mary's Catholic zeal.--Her moderation at first.--Mary's terrible persecution of the Protestants.--Burning at the stake.--The title of Bloody given to Mary.--Mary and Elizabeth reconciled.--Scenes of festivity.--The war with France.--Loss of Calais.--Murmurs of the English.--King of Sweden's proposal to Elizabeth.--Mary's energy.--Mary's privy council alarmed.--Their perplexity.--Uncertainty about Elizabeth's future course.--Her cautious policy.--Death of Mary.--Announcement to Parliament.--Elizabeth proclaimed.--Joy of the people.--The Te Deum.--Elizabeth's emotions.--Cecil made secretary of state.--His faithfulness.--Elizabeth's charge to Cecil.--Her journey to London.--Elizabeth's triumphant entrance into the Tower.--The coronation.--Pageants in the streets.--Devices.--Presentation of the Bible.--The heavy purse.--The sprig of rosemary.--The wedding ring.

If it were the story of Mary instead of that of Elizabeth that we were following, we should have now to pause and draw a very melancholy picture of the scenes which darkened the close of the queen's unfortunate and unhappy history. Mary loved her husband, but she could not secure his love in return. He treated her with supercilious coldness and neglect, and evinced, from time to time, a degree of interest in other ladies which awakened her jealousy and anger. Of all the terrible convulsions to which the human soul is subject, there is not one which agitates it more deeply than the tumult of feeling produced by the mingling of resentment and love. Such a mingling, or, rather, such a conflict, between passions apparently inconsistent with each other, is generally considered not possible by those who have never experienced it. But it is possible. It is possible to be stung with a sense of the ingratitude, and selfishness, and cruelty of an object, which, after all, the heart will persist in clinging to with the fondest affection. Vexation and anger, a burning sense of injury, and desire for revenge, on the one hand, and feelings of love, resistless and uncontrollable, and bearing, in their turn, all before them, alternately get possession of the soul, harrowing and devastating it in their awful conflict, and even sometimes reigning over it, for a time, in a temporary but dreadful calm, like that of two wrestlers who pause a moment, exhausted in a mortal combat, but grappling each other with deadly energy all the time, while they are taking breath for a renewal of the conflict. Queen Mary, in one of these paroxysms, seized a portrait of her husband and tore it into shreds. The reader, who has his or her experience in affairs of the heart yet to come, will say, perhaps, her love for him then must have been all gone. No; it was at its height. We do not tear the portraits of those who are indifferent to us.

At the beginning of her reign, and, in fact, during all the previous periods of her life, Mary had been an honest and conscientious Catholic. She undoubtedly truly believed that the Christian Church ought to be banded together in one great communion, with the Pope of Rome as its spiritual head, and that her father had broken away from this communion--which was, in fact, strictly true--merely to obtain a pretext for getting released from her mother. How natural, under such circumstances, that she should have desired to return. She commenced, immediately on her accession, a course of measures to bring the nation back to the Roman Catholic communion. She managed very prudently and cautiously at first--especially while the affair of her marriage was pending--seemingly very desirous of doing nothing to exasperate those who were of the Protestant faith, or even to awaken their opposition. After she was married, however, her desire to please her Catholic husband, and his widely-extended and influential circle of Catholic friends on the Continent, made her more eager to press forward the work of putting down the Reformation in England; and as her marriage was now effected, she was less concerned about the consequences of any opposition which she might excite. Then, besides, her temper, never very sweet, was sadly soured by her husband's treatment of her. She vented her ill will upon those who would not yield to her wishes in respect to their religious faith. She caused more and more severe laws to be passed, and enforced them by more and more severe penalties. The more she pressed these violent measures, the more the fortitude and resolution of those who suffered from them were aroused. And, on the other hand, the more they resisted, the more determined she became that she would compel them to submit. She went on from one mode of coercion to another, until she reached the last possible point, and inflicted the most dreadful physical suffering which it is possible for man to inflict upon his fellow-man.

This worst and most terrible injury is to burn the living victim in a fire. That a woman could ever order this to be done would seem to be incredible. Queen Mary, however, and her government, were so determined to put down, at all hazards, all open disaffection to the Catholic cause, that they did not give up the contest until they had burned nearly three hundred persons by fire, of whom more than fifty were women, and four were children! This horrible persecution was, however, of no avail. Dissentients increased faster than they could be burned; and such dreadful punishments became at last so intolerably odious to the nation that they were obliged to desist, and then the various ministers of state concerned in them attempted to throw off the blame upon each other. The English nation have never forgiven Mary for these atrocities. They gave her the name of Bloody Mary at the time, and she has retained it to the present day. In one of the ancient histories of the realm, at the head of the chapter devoted to Mary, there is placed, as an appropriate emblem of the character of her reign, the picture of a man writhing helplessly at a stake, with the flames curling around him, and a ferocious-looking soldier standing by, stirring up the fire.

The various disappointments, vexations, and trials which Mary endured toward the close of her life, had one good effect; they softened the animosity which she had felt toward Elizabeth, and in the end something like a friendship seemed to spring up between the sisters. Abandoned by her husband, and looked upon with dislike or hatred by her subjects, and disappointed in all her plans, she seemed to turn at last to Elizabeth for companionship and comfort. The sisters visited each other. First Elizabeth went to London to visit the queen, and was received with great ceremony and parade. Then the queen went to Hatfield to visit the princess, attended by a large company of ladies and gentlemen of the court, and several days were spent there in festivities and rejoicings. There were plays in the palace, and a bear-baiting in the court-yard, and hunting in the park, and many other schemes of pleasure. This renewal of friendly intercourse between the queen and the princess brought the latter gradually out of her retirement. Now that the queen began to evince a friendly spirit toward her, it was safe for others to show her kindness and to pay her attention. The disposition to do this increased rapidly as Mary's health gradually declined, and it began to be understood that she would not live long, and that, consequently, Elizabeth would soon be called to the throne.

The war which Mary had been drawn into with France, by Philip's threat that he would never see her again, proved very disastrous. The town of Calais, which is opposite to Dover, across the straits, and, of course, on the French side of the channel, had been in the possession of the English for two hundred years. It was very gratifying to English pride to hold possession of such a stronghold on the French shore; but now every thing seemed to go against Mary. Calais was defended by a citadel nearly as large as the town itself, and was deemed impregnable. In addition to this, an enormous English force was concentrated there. The French general, however, contrived, partly by stratagem, and partly by overpowering numbers of troops, and ships, and batteries of cannon, to get possession of the whole. The English nation were indignant at this result. Their queen and her government, so energetic in imprisoning and burning her own subjects at home, were powerless, it seemed, in coping with their enemies abroad. Murmurs of dissatisfaction were heard every where, and Mary sank down upon her sick bed overwhelmed with disappointment, vexation, and chagrin. She said that she should die, and that if, after her death, they examined her body, they would find Calais like a load upon her heart.

In the mean time, it must have been Elizabeth's secret wish that she would die, since her death would release the princess from all the embarrassments and restraints of her position, and raise her at once to the highest pinnacle of honor and power. She remained, however, quietly at Hatfield, acting in all things in a very discreet and cautious manner. At one time she received proposals from the King of Sweden that she would accept of his son as her husband. She asked the embassador if he had communicated the affair to Mary. On his replying that he had not, Elizabeth said that she could not entertain at all any such question, unless her sister were first consulted and should give her approbation. She acted on the same principles in every thing, being very cautious to give Mary and her government no cause of complaint against her, and willing to wait patiently until her own time should come.

Though Mary's disappointments and losses filled her mind with anguish and suffering, they did not soften her heart. She seemed to grow more cruel and vindictive the more her plans and projects failed. Adversity vexed and irritated, instead of calming and subduing her. She revived her persecutions of the Protestants. She fitted out a fleet of a hundred and twenty ships to make a descent upon the French coast, and attempt to retrieve her fallen fortunes there. She called Parliament together and asked for more supplies. All this time she was confined to her sick chamber, but not considered in danger. The Parliament were debating the question of supplies. Her privy council were holding daily meetings to carry out the plans and schemes which she still continued to form, and all was excitement and bustle in and around the court, when one day the council was thunderstruck by an announcement that she was dying.

They knew very well that her death would be a terrible blow to them. They were all Catholics, and had been Mary's instruments in the terrible persecutions with which she had oppressed the Protestant faith. With Mary's death, of course they would fall. A Protestant princess was ready, at Hatfield, to ascend the throne. Every thing would be changed, and there was even danger that they might, in their turn, be sent to the stake, in retaliation for the cruelties which they had caused others to suffer. They made arrangements to have Mary's death, whenever it should take place, concealed for a few hours, till they could consider what they should do.

There was nothing that they could do. There was now no other considerable claimant to the throne but Elizabeth, except Mary Queen of Scots, who was far away in France. She was a Catholic, it was true; but to bring her into the country and place her upon the throne seemed to be a hopeless undertaking. Queen Mary's counselors soon found that they must give up their cause in despair. Any attempt to resist Elizabeth's claims would be high treason, and, of course, if unsuccessful, would bring the heads of all concerned in it to the block.

Besides, it was not certain that Elizabeth would act decidedly as a Protestant. She had been very prudent and cautious during Mary's reign, and had been very careful never to manifest any hostility to the Catholics. She never had acted as Mary had done on the occasion of her brother's funeral, when she refused even to countenance with her presence the national service because it was under Protestant forms. Elizabeth had always accompanied Mary to mass whenever occasion required; she had always spoken respectfully of the Catholic faith; and once she asked Mary to lend her some Catholic books, in order that she might inform herself more fully on the subject of the principles of the Roman faith. It is true, she acted thus not because there was any real leaning in her mind toward the Catholic religion; it was all merely a wise and sagacious policy. Surrounded by difficulties and dangers as she was during Mary's reign, her only hope of safety was in passing as quietly as possible along, and managing warily, so as to keep the hostility which was burning secretly against her from breaking out into an open flame. This was her object in retiring so much from the court and from all participation in public affairs, in avoiding all religious and political contests, and spending her time in the study of Greek, and Latin, and philosophy. The consequence was, that when Mary died, nobody knew certainly what course Elizabeth would pursue.

Nobody had any strong motive for opposing her succession. The council, therefore, after a short consultation, concluded to do nothing but simply to send a message to the House of Lords, announcing to them the unexpected death of the queen.

The House of Lords, on receiving this intelligence, sent for the Commons to come into their hall, as is usual when any important communication is to be made to them either by the Lords themselves or by the sovereign. The chancellor, who is the highest civil officer of the kingdom in respect to rank, and who presides in the House of Lords, clothed in a magnificent antique costume, then rose and announced to the Commons, standing before him, the death of the sovereign. There was a moment's solemn pause, such as propriety on the occasion of an announcement like this required, all thoughts being, too, for a moment turned to the chamber where the body of the departed queen was lying. But the sovereignty was no longer there. The mysterious principle had fled with the parting breath, and Elizabeth, though wholly unconscious of it, had been for several hours the queen. The thoughts, therefore, of the august and solemn assembly lingered but for a moment in the royal palace, which had now lost all its glory; they soon turned spontaneously, and with eager haste, to the new sovereign at Hatfield, and the lofty arches of the Parliament hall rung with loud acclamations, "God save Queen Elizabeth, and grant her a long and happy reign."

The members of the Parliament went forth immediately to proclaim the new queen. There are two principal places where it was then customary to proclaim the English sovereigns. One of these was before the royal palace at Westminster, and the other in the city of London, at a very public place called the Great Cross at Cheapside. The people assembled in great crowds at these points to witness the ceremony, and received the announcement which the heralds made, with the most ardent expressions of joy. The bells were every where rung; tables were spread in the streets, and booths erected, bonfires and illuminations were prepared for the evening, and every thing indicated a deep and universal joy.

In fact, this joy was so strongly expressed as to be even in some degree disrespectful to the memory of the departed queen. There is a famous ancient Latin hymn which has long been sung in England and on the Continent of Europe on occasions of great public rejoicing. It is called the Te Deum, or sometimes the Te Deum Laudamus. These last are the three Latin words with which the hymn commences, and mean, Thee, God, we praise. They sung the Te Deum in the churches of London on the Sunday after Mary died.

In the mean time, messengers from the council proceeded with all speed to Hatfield, to announce to Elizabeth the death of her sister, and her own accession to the sovereign power. The tidings, of course, filled Elizabeth's mind with the deepest emotions. The oppressive sense of constraint and danger which she had endured as her daily burden for so many years, was lifted suddenly from her soul. She could not but rejoice, though she was too much upon her guard to express her joy. She was overwhelmed with a profound agitation, and, kneeling down, she exclaimed in Latin, "It is the Lord's doing, and it is wonderful in our eyes."

Several of the members of Mary's privy council repaired immediately to Hatfield. The queen summoned them to attend her, and in their presence appointed her chief secretary of state. His name was Sir William Cecil. He was a man of great learning and ability, and he remained in office under Elizabeth for forty years. He became her chief adviser and instrument, an able, faithful, and indefatigable servant and friend during almost the whole of her reign. His name is accordingly indissolubly connected with that of Elizabeth in all the political events which occurred while she continued upon the throne, and it will, in consequence, very frequently occur in the sequel of this history. He was now about forty years of age. Elizabeth was twenty-five.

Elizabeth had known Cecil long before. He had been a faithful and true friend to her in her adversity. He had been, in many cases, a confidential adviser, and had maintained a secret correspondence with her in certain trying periods of her life. She had resolved, doubtless, to make him her chief secretary of state so soon as she should succeed to the throne. And now that the time had arrived, she instated him solemnly in his office. In so doing, she pronounced, in the hearing of the other members of the council, the following charge:

"I give you this charge that you shall be of my privy council, and content yourself to take pains for me and my realm. This judgment I have of you, that you will not be corrupted with any gift; and that you will be faithful to the state; and that, without respect of my private will, you will give me that counsel that you think best; and that, if you shall know any thing necessary to be declared to me of secrecy you shall show it to myself only; and assure yourself I will not fail to keep taciturnity therein. And therefore herewith I charge you."

It was about a week after the death of Mary before the arrangements were completed for Elizabeth's journey to London, to take possession of the castles and palaces which pertain there to the English sovereigns. She was followed on this journey by a train of about a thousand attendants, all nobles or personages of high rank, both gentlemen and ladies. She went first to a palace called the Charter House, near London, where she stopped until preparations could be made for her formal and public entrance into the Tower; not, as before, through the Traitors' Gate, a prisoner, but openly, through the grand entrance, in the midst of acclamations as the proud and applauded sovereign of the mighty realm whose capital the ancient fortress was stationed to defend. The streets through which the gorgeous procession was to pass were spread with fine, smooth gravel; bands of musicians were stationed at intervals, and decorated arches, and banners, and flags, with countless devices of loyalty and welcome, and waving handkerchiefs, greeted her all the way. Heralds and other great officers, magnificently dressed, and mounted on horses richly caparisoned, rode before her, announcing her approach, with trumpets and proclamations; while she followed in the train, mounted upon a beautiful horse, the object of universal homage. Thus Elizabeth entered the Tower; and inasmuch as forgetting her friends is a fault with which she can not justly be charged, we may hope, at least, that one of the first acts which she performed, after getting established in the royal apartments, was to send for and reward the kind-hearted child who had been reprimanded for bringing her the flowers.

The coronation, when the time arrived for it, was very splendid. The queen went in state in a sumptuous chariot, preceded by trumpeters and heralds in armor, and accompanied by a long train of noblemen, barons, and gentlemen, and also of ladies, all most richly dressed in crimson velvet, the trappings of the horses being of the same material. The people of London thronged all the streets through which she was to pass, and made the air resound with shouts and acclamations. There were triumphal arches erected here and there on the way, with a great variety of odd and quaint devices, and a child stationed upon each, who explained the devices to Elizabeth as she passed, in English verse, written for the occasion. One of these pageants was entitled "The Seat of worthy Governance." There was a throne, supported by figures which represented the cardinal virtues, such as Piety, Wisdom, Temperance, Industry, Truth, and beneath their feet were the opposite vices, Superstition, Ignorance, Intemperance, Idleness, and Falsehood: these the virtues were trampling upon. On the throne was a representation of Elizabeth. At one place were eight personages dressed to represent the eight beatitudes pronounced by our Savior in his sermon on the Mount--the meek, the merciful, &c. Each of these qualities was ingeniously ascribed to Elizabeth. This could be done with much more propriety then than in subsequent years. In another place, an ancient figure, representing Time, came out of a cave which had been artificially constructed with great ingenuity, leading his daughter, whose name was Truth. Truth had an English Bible in her hands, which she presented to Elizabeth as she passed. This had a great deal of meaning; for the Catholic government of Mary had discouraged the circulation of the Scriptures in the vernacular tongue. When the procession arrived in the middle of the city, some officers of the city government approached the queen's chariot, and delivered to her a present of a very large and heavy purse filled with gold. The queen had to employ both hands in lifting it in. It contained an amount equal in value to two or three thousand dollars.

The queen was very affable and gracious to all the people on the way. Poor women would come up to her carriage and offer her flowers, which she would very condescendingly accept. Several times she stopped her carriage when she saw that any one wished to speak with her, or had something to offer; and so great was the exaltation of a queen in those days, in the estimation of mankind, that these acts were considered by all the humble citizens of London as acts of very extraordinary affability, and they awakened universal enthusiasm. There was one branch of rosemary given to the queen by a poor woman in Fleet Street; the queen put it up conspicuously in the carriage, where it remained all the way, watched by ten thousand eyes, till it got to Westminster.

The coronation took place at Westminster on the following day. The crown was placed upon the young maiden's head in the midst of a great throng of ladies and gentlemen, who were all superbly dressed, and who made the vast edifice in which the service was performed ring with their acclamations and their shouts of "Long live the Queen!" During the ceremonies, Elizabeth placed a wedding ring upon her finger with great formality, to denote that she considered the occasion as the celebration of her espousal to the realm of England; she was that day a bride, and should never have, she said, any other husband. She kept this, the only wedding ring she ever wore, upon her finger, without once removing it, for more than forty years.

CHAPTER VII.

THE WAR IN SCOTLAND.

1559-1560

Elizabeth and Mary Queen of Scots.--Their rivalry.--Character of Mary.--Character of Elizabeth.--Elizabeth's celebrity while living.--Interest in Mary when dead.--Real nature of the question at issue between Mary and Elizabeth.--The two marriages.--One or the other necessarily null.--Views of Mary's friends.--Views of Elizabeth's friends.--Circumstances of Henry the Eighth's first marriage.--The papal dispensation.--Doubts about it.--England turns Protestant.--The marriage annulled.--Mary in France.--She becomes Queen of France.--Mary's pretensions to the English crown.--Elizabeth's fears.--Measures of Elizabeth.--Progress of Protestantism in Scotland.--Difficulties in

Scotland.--Elizabeth's interference.--Fruitless negotiations.--The war goes on.--The French shut up in Leith.--Situation of the town.--The English victorious.--The Treaty of Edinburgh.--Stipulations of the treaty.--Mary refuses to ratify it.--Death of Mary's husband.--She returns to Scotland.

Queen Elizabeth and Mary Queen of Scots are strongly associated together in the minds of all readers of English history. They were cotemporary sovereigns, reigning at the same time over sister kingdoms. They were cousins, and yet, precisely on account of the family relationship which existed between them, they became implacable foes. The rivalry and hostility, sometimes open and sometimes concealed, was always in action, and, after a contest of more than twenty years, Elizabeth triumphed. She made Mary her prisoner, kept her many years a captive, and at last closed the contest by commanding, or at least allowing, her fallen rival to be beheaded.

Thus Elizabeth had it all her own way while the scenes of her life and of Mary's were transpiring, but since that time mankind have generally sympathized most strongly with the conquered one, and condemned the conqueror. There are several reasons for this, and among them is the vast influence exerted by the difference in the personal character of the parties. Mary was beautiful, feminine in spirit, and lovely. Elizabeth was talented, masculine, and plain. Mary was artless, unaffected, and gentle. Elizabeth was heartless, intriguing, and insincere. With Mary, though her ruling principle was ambition, her ruling passion was love. Her love led her to great transgressions and into many sorrows, but mankind pardon the sins and pity the sufferings which are caused by love more readily than those of any other origin. With Elizabeth, ambition was the ruling principle, and the ruling passion too. Love, with her, was only a pastime. Her transgressions were the cool, deliberate, well-considered acts of selfishness and desire of power. During her life-time her success secured her the applauses of the world. The world is always ready to glorify the greatness which rises visibly before it, and to forget sufferings which are meekly and patiently borne in seclusion and solitude. Men praised and honored Elizabeth, therefore, while she lived, and neglected Mary. But since the halo and the fascination of the visible greatness and glory have passed away, they have found a far greater charm in Mary's beauty and misfortune than in her great rival's pride and power.

There is often thus a great difference in the comparative interest we take in persons or scenes, when, on the one hand, they are realities before our eyes, and when, on the other, they are only imaginings which are brought to our minds by pictures or descriptions. The hardships which it was very disagreeable or painful to bear, afford often great amusement or pleasure in the recollection. The old broken gate which a gentleman would not tolerate an hour upon his grounds, is a great beauty in the picture which hangs in his parlor. We shun poverty and distress while they are actually existing; nothing is more disagreeable to us; and we gaze upon prosperity and wealth with never-ceasing pleasure. But when they are gone, and we have only the tale to hear, it is the story of sorrow and suffering which possesses the charm. Thus it happened that when the two queens were living realities, Elizabeth was the center of attraction and the object of universal homage; but when they came to be themes of history, all eyes and hearts began soon to turn instinctively to Mary. It was London, and Westminster, and Kenilworth that possessed the interest while Elizabeth lived, but it is Holyrood and Loch Leven now.

It results from these causes that Mary's story is read far more frequently than Elizabeth's, and this operates still further to the advantage of the former, for we are always prone to take sides with the heroine of the tale we are reading. All these considerations, which have had so much influence on the judgment men form, or, rather, on the feeling to which they incline in this famous contest, have, it must be confessed, very little to do with the true merits of the case. And if we make a serious attempt to lay all such considerations aside, and to look into the controversy with cool and rigid impartiality, we shall find it very difficult to arrive at any satisfactory conclusion. There are two questions to be decided. In advancing their conflicting claims to the English crown, was it Elizabeth or Mary that was in the right? If Elizabeth was right, were the measures which she resorted to to secure her own rights, and to counteract Mary's pretensions, politically justifiable? We do not propose to add our own to the hundred decisions which various writers have given to this question, but only to narrate the facts, and leave each reader to come to his own conclusions.

The foundation of the long and dreadful quarrel between these royal cousins was, as has been already remarked, their consanguinity, which made them both competitors for the same throne; and as that throne was, in some respects, the highest and most powerful in the world, it is not surprising that two such ambitious women should be eager and persevering in their contest for it. By turning to the genealogical table on page 68, where a view is presented of the royal family of England in the time of Elizabeth, the reader will see once more what was the precise relationship which the two queens bore to each other and to the succession. By this table it is very evident that Elizabeth was the true inheritor of the crown, provided it were admitted that she was the lawful daughter and heir of King Henry the Eighth, and this depended on the question of the validity of her father's marriage with his first wife, Catharine of Aragon; for, as has been before said, he was married to Anne Boleyn before obtaining any thing like a divorce from Catharine; consequently, the marriage with Elizabeth's mother could not be legally valid, unless that with Catharine had been void from the beginning. The friends of Mary Queen of Scots maintained that it was not thus void, and that, consequently, the marriage with Anne Boleyn was null; that Elizabeth, therefore, the descendant of the marriage, was not, legally and technically, a daughter of Henry the Eighth, and, consequently, not entitled to inherit his crown; and that the crown, of right, ought to descend to the next heir, that is, to Mary Queen of Scots herself.

Queen Elizabeth's friends and partisans maintained, on the other hand, that the marriage of King Henry with Catharine was null and void from the beginning, because Catharine had been before the wife of his brother. The circumstances of this marriage were very curious and peculiar. It was his father's work, and not his own. His father was King Henry the Seventh. Henry the Seventh had several children, and among them were his two oldest sons, Arthur and Henry. When Arthur was about sixteen years old, his father, being very much in want of money, conceived the plan of replenishing his coffers by marrying his son to a rich wife. He accordingly contracted a marriage between him and Catharine of Aragon, Catharine's father agreeing to pay him two hundred thousand crowns as her dowry. The juvenile bridegroom enjoyed the honors and pleasures of married life for a few months, and then died.

This event was a great domestic calamity to the king, not because he mourned the loss of his son, but that he could not bear the idea of the loss of the dowry. By the law and usage in such cases, he was bound not only to forego the payment of the other half of the dowry, but he had himself no right to retain the half that he had already received. While his son lived, being a minor, the father might, not improperly, hold the money in his son's name; but when he died this right ceased, and as Arthur left no child, Henry perceived that he should be obliged to pay back the money. To avoid this unpleasant necessity, the king conceived the plan of marrying the youthful widow again to his second boy, Henry, who was about a year younger than Arthur, and he made proposals to this effect to the King of Aragon.

The King of Aragon made no objection to this proposal, except that it was a thing unheard of among Christian nations, or heard of only to be condemned, for a man or even a boy to marry his brother's widow. All laws, human and divine, were clear and absolute against this. Still, if the dispensation of the pope could be obtained, he would make no objection. Catharine might espouse the second boy, and he would allow the one hundred thousand crowns already paid to stand, and would also pay the other hundred thousand. The dispensation was accordingly obtained, and every thing made ready for the marriage.

Very soon after this, however, and before the new marriage was carried into effect, King Henry the Seventh died, and this second boy, now the oldest son, though only about seventeen years of age, ascended the throne as King Henry the Eighth. There was great discussion and debate, soon after his accession, whether the marriage which his father had arranged should proceed. Some argued that no papal dispensation could authorize or justify such a marriage. Others maintained that a papal dispensation could legalize any thing; for it is a doctrine of the Catholic Church that the pope has a certain discretionary power over all laws, human and divine, under the authority given to his great predecessor, the Apostle Peter, by the words of Christ: "Whatsoever thou shalt bind on earth shall be bound in heaven, and whatsoever thou shalt loose on earth shall be loosed in heaven."[C] Henry seems not to have puzzled his head at all with the legal question; he wanted to have the young widow for his wife, and he settled the affair on that ground alone. They were married.

[Footnote C: Matthew, xvi. 19]

Catharine was a faithful and dutiful spouse; but when, at last, Henry fell in love with Anne Boleyn, he made these old difficulties a pretext for discarding her. He endeavored, as has been already related, to induce the papal authorities to annul their dispensation; because they would not do it, he espoused the Protestant cause, and England, as a nation, seceded from the Catholic communion. The ecclesiastical and parliamentary authorities of his own realm then, being made Protestant, annulled the marriage, and thus Anne Boleyn, to whom he had previously been married by a private ceremony, became legally and technically his wife. If this annulling of his first marriage were valid, then Elizabeth was his heir--otherwise not; for if the pope's dispensation was to stand, then Catharine was a wife. Anne Boleyn would in that case, of course, have been only a companion, and Elizabeth, claiming through her, a usurper.

The question, thus, was very complicated. It branched into extensive ramifications, which opened a wide field of debate, and led to endless controversies. It is not probable, however, that Mary Queen of Scots, or her friends, gave themselves much trouble about the legal points at issue. She and they were all Catholics, and it was sufficient for them to know that the Holy Father at Rome had sanctioned the marriage of Catharine, and that that marriage, if allowed to stand, made her the Queen of England. She was at this time in France. She had been sent there at a very early period of her life, to escape the troubles of her native land, and also to be educated. She was a gentle and beautiful child, and as she grew up amid the gay scenes and festivities of Paris, she became a very great favorite, being universally beloved. She married at length, though while she was still quite young, the son of the

French king. Her young husband became king himself soon afterward, on account of his father's being killed, in a very remarkable manner, at a tournament; and thus Mary, Queen of Scots before, became also Queen of France now. All these events, passed over thus very summarily here, are narrated in full detail in the History of Mary Queen of Scots pertaining to this series.

While Mary was thus residing in France as the wife of the king, she was surrounded by a very large and influential circle, who were Catholics like herself, and who were also enemies of Elizabeth and of England, and glad to find any pretext for disturbing her reign. These persons brought forward Mary's claim. They persuaded Mary that she was fairly entitled to the English crown. They awakened her youthful ambition, and excited strong desires in her heart to attain to the high elevation of Queen of England. Mary at length assumed the title in some of her official acts, and combined the arms of England with those of Scotland in the escutcheons with which her furniture and her plate were emblazoned.

When Queen Elizabeth learned that Mary was advancing such pretensions to her crown, she was made very uneasy by it. There was, perhaps, no immediate danger, but then there was a very large Catholic party in England, and they would naturally espouse Mary's cause and they might, at some future time, gather strength so as to make Elizabeth a great deal of trouble. She accordingly sent an embassador over to France to remonstrate against Mary's advancing these pretensions. But she could get no satisfactory reply. Mary would not disavow her claim to Elizabeth's crown, nor would she directly assert it. Elizabeth, then, knowing that all her danger lay in the power and influence of her own Catholic subjects, went to work, very cautiously and warily, but in a very extended and efficient way, to establish the Reformation, and to undermine and destroy all traces of Catholic power. She proceeded in this work with great circumspection, so as not to excite opposition or alarm.

In the mean time, the Protestant cause was making progress in Scotland too, by its own inherent energies, and against the influence of the government.

Finally, the Scotch Protestants organized themselves, and commenced an open rebellion against the regent whom Mary had left in power while she was away. They sent to Elizabeth to come and aid them. Mary and her friends in France sent French troops to assist the government. Elizabeth hesitated very much whether to comply with the request of the rebels. It is very dangerous for a sovereign to countenance rebellion in any way. Then she shrunk, too, from the expense which she foresaw that such an attempt would involve. To fit out a fleet, and to levy and equip an army, and to continue the forces thus raised in action during a long and uncertain campaign, would cost a large sum of money, and Elizabeth was constitutionally economical and frugal. But then, on the other hand, as she deliberated upon the affair long and, anxiously, both alone and with her council, she thought that, if she should so far succeed as to get the government of Scotland into her power, she could compel Mary to renounce forever all claims to the English crown, by threatening her, if she would not do it, with the loss of her own.

Finally, she decided on making the attempt. Cecil, her wise and prudent counselor, strongly advised it. He said it was far better to carry on the contest with Mary and the French in one of their countries than in her own. She began to make preparations. Mary and the French government, on learning this, were alarmed in their turn. They sent word to Elizabeth that for her to render countenance and aid to rebels in arms against their sovereign, in a sister kingdom, was wholly unjustifiable, and they remonstrated most earnestly against it. Besides making this remonstrance, they offered, as an inducement of another kind, that if she would refrain from taking any part in the contest in Scotland, they would restore to her the great town and citadel of Calais, which her sister had been so much grieved to lose. To this Elizabeth replied that, so long as Mary adhered to her pretensions to the English crown, she should be compelled to take energetic measures to protect herself from them; and as to Calais, the possession of a fishing town on a foreign coast was of no moment to her in comparison with the peace and security of her own realm. This answer did not tend to close the breach. Besides the bluntness of the refusal of their offer, the French were irritated and vexed to hear their famous sea-port spoken of so contemptuously.

Elizabeth accordingly fitted out a fleet and an army, and sent them northward. A French fleet, with re-enforcements for Mary's adherents in this contest, set sail from France at about the same time. It was a very important question to be determined which of these two fleets should get first upon the stage of action.

In the mean time, the Protestant party in Scotland, or the rebels, as Queen Mary and her government called them, had had very hard work to maintain their ground. There was a large French force already there, and their co-operation and aid made the government too strong for the insurgents to resist. But, when Elizabeth's English army crossed the frontier, the face of affairs was changed. The French forces retreated in their turn. The English army advanced. The Scotch Protestants came forth from the recesses of the Highlands to which they had retreated, and, drawing closer and closer around the French and the government forces, they hemmed them in more and more narrowly, and at last shut them up in the ancient town of Leith, to which they retreated in search of a temporary shelter, until the French fleet, with re-enforcements, should arrive.

The town of Leith is on the shore of the Firth of Forth, not far from Edinburgh. It is the port or landing-place of Edinburgh, in approaching it from the sea. It is on the southern shore of the firth, and Edinburgh stands on higher land, about two miles south of it. Leith was strongly fortified in those days, and the French army felt very secure there, though yet anxiously awaiting the arrival of the fleet which was to release them. The English army advanced in the mean time, eager to get possession of the city before the expected succors should arrive. The English made an assault upon the walls. The French, with desperate bravery, repelled it. The French made a sortie; that is, they rushed out of a sudden and attacked the English lines. The English concentrated their forces at the point attacked, and drove them back again. These struggles continued, both sides very eager for victory, and both watching all the time for the appearance of a fleet in the offing.

At length, one day, a cloud of white sails appeared rounding the point of land which forms the southern boundary of the firth, and the French were thrown at once into the highest state of exultation and excitement. But this pleasure was soon turned into disappointment and chagrin by finding that it was Elizabeth's fleet, and not theirs, which was coming into view. This ended the contest. The French fleet never arrived. It was dispersed and destroyed by a storm. The besieged army sent out a flag of truce, proposing to suspend hostilities until the terms of a treaty could be agreed upon. The truce was granted. Commissioners were appointed on each side. These commissioners met at Edinburgh, and agreed upon the terms of a permanent peace. The treaty, which is called in history the Treaty of Edinburgh, was solemnly signed by the commissioners appointed to make it, and then transmitted to England and to France to be ratified by the respective queens. Queen Elizabeth's forces and the French forces were then both, as the treaty provided, immediately withdrawn. The dispute, too, between the Protestants and the Catholics in Scotland was also settled, though it is not necessary for our purpose in this narrative to explain particularly in what way.

There was one point, however, in the stipulations of this treaty which is of essential importance in this narrative, and that is, that it was agreed that Mary should relinquish all claims whatever to the English crown so long as Elizabeth lived. This, in fact, was the essential point in the whole transaction. Mary, it is true, was not present to agree to it; but the commissioners agreed to it in her name, and it was stipulated that Mary should solemnly ratify the treaty as soon as it could be sent to her.

But Mary would not ratify it--at least so far as this last article was concerned. She said that she had no intention of doing any thing to molest Elizabeth in her possession of the throne, but that as to herself, whatever rights might legally and justly belong to her, she could not consent to sign them away. The other articles of the treaty had, however, in the mean time, brought the war to a close, and both the French and English armies were withdrawn. Neither party had any inclination to renew the conflict; but yet, so far as the great question between Mary and Elizabeth was concerned, the difficulty was as far from being settled as ever. In fact, it was in a worse position than before; for, in addition to her other grounds of complaint against Mary, Elizabeth now charged her with dishonorably refusing to be bound by a compact which had been solemnly made in her name, by agents whom she had fully authorized to make it.

It was about this time that Mary's husband, the King of France, died, and, after enduring various trials and troubles in France, Mary concluded to return to her own realm. She sent to Elizabeth to get a safe-conduct--a sort of permission allowing her to pass unmolested through the English seas. Elizabeth refused to grant it unless Mary would first ratify the treaty of Edinburgh. This Mary would not do, but undertook, rather, to get home without the permission. Elizabeth sent ships to intercept her; but Mary's little squadron, when they approached the shore, were hidden by a fog, and so she got safe to land. After this there was quiet between Mary and Elizabeth for many years, but no peace.

CHAPTER VIII.

ELIZABETH'S LOVERS.

1560-1581

Claimants to the throne.--General character of Elizabeth's reign.--Elizabeth's suitors.--Their motives.--Philip of Spain proposes.--His strange conduct.--Elizabeth declines Philip's proposal.--Her reasons for so doing.--The English people wish Elizabeth to be married.--Petition of the Parliament.--Elizabeth's "gracious" reply.--Elizabeth attacked with the small-pox.--Alarm of the country.--The Earl of Leicester.--His character.--Services of Cecil.--Elizabeth's attachment to Leicester.--Leicester's wife.--Her mysterious death.--Leicester hated by the people.--Various rumors.--The torch-light conversation.--The servants quarrel.--Splendid style of living.--Public ceremonies.--Elizabeth recommends Leicester to Mary Queen of Scots.--Mary marries Darnley.--Elizabeth's visit to Kenilworth.--Leicester's marriage.--Elizabeth sends him to prison.--Prosperity of Elizabeth's reign.--The Duke of Anjou.--Catharine de Medici.--She proposes her son to Elizabeth.--Quarrels of the favorites.--The shot.--The people oppose the match.--The arrangements completed.--The match broken off.--The duke's rage.--The duke's departure.--The farewell.

Elizabeth was now securely established upon her throne. It is true that Mary Queen of Scots had not renounced her pretensions, but there was no immediate prospect of her making any attempt to realize them, and very little hope for her that she would be successful, if she were to undertake it. There were other claimants, it is true, but their claims were more remote and doubtful than Mary's. These conflicting pretensions were likely to make the country some trouble after Elizabeth's death, but there was very slight probability that they would sensibly molest Elizabeth's possession of the throne during her life-time, though they caused her no little anxiety.

The reign which Elizabeth thus commenced was one of the longest, most brilliant, and, in many respects, the most prosperous in the whole series presented to our view in the long succession of English sovereigns. Elizabeth continued a queen for forty-five years, during all which time she remained a single lady; and she died, at last, a venerable maiden, seventy years of age.

It was not for want of lovers, or, rather, of admirers and suitors, that Elizabeth lived single all her days. During the first twenty years of her reign, one half of her history is a history of matrimonial schemes and negotiations. It seemed as if all the marriageable princes and potentates of Europe were seized, one after another, with a desire to share her seat upon the English throne. They tried every possible means to win her consent. They dispatched embassadors; they opened long negotiations; they sent her ship-loads of the most expensive presents: some of the nobles of high rank in her own realm expended their vast estates, and reduced themselves to poverty, in vain attempts to please her. Elizabeth, like any other woman, loved these attentions. They pleased her vanity, and gratified those instinctive impulses of the female heart by which woman is fitted for happiness and love. Elizabeth encouraged the hopes of those who addressed her sufficiently to keep them from giving up in despair and abandoning her. And in one or two cases she seemed to come very near yielding. But it always happened that, when the time arrived in which a final decision must be made, ambition and desire of power proved stronger than love, and she preferred continuing to occupy her lofty position by herself, alone.

Philip of Spain, the husband of her sister Mary, was the first of these suitors. He had seen Elizabeth a good deal in England during his residence there, and had even taken her part in her difficulties with Mary, and had exerted his influence to have her released from her confinement. As soon as Mary died and Elizabeth was proclaimed, one of her first acts was, as was very proper, to send an embassador to Flanders to inform the bereaved husband of his loss. It is a curious illustration of the degree and kind of affection that Philip had borne to his departed wife, that immediately on receiving intelligence of her death by Elizabeth's embassador, he sent a special dispatch to his own embassador in London to make a proposal to Elizabeth to take him for her husband!

Elizabeth decided very soon to decline this proposal. She had ostensible reasons, and real reasons for this. The chief ostensible reason was, that Philip was so inveterately hated by all the English people, and Elizabeth was extremely desirous of being popular. She relied solely on the loyalty and faithfulness of her Protestant subjects to maintain her rights to the succession, and she knew that if she displeased them by such an unpopular Catholic marriage, her reliance upon them must be very much weakened. They might even abandon her entirely. The reason, therefore, that she assigned publicly was, that Philip was a Catholic, and that the connection could not, on that account, be agreeable to the English people.

Among the real reasons was one of a very peculiar nature. It happened that there was an objection to her marriage with Philip similar to the one urged against that of Henry with Catharine of Aragon. Catharine had been the wife of Henry's brother. Philip had been the husband of Elizabeth's sister. Now Philip had offered to procure the pope's dispensation, by which means this difficulty would be surmounted. But then all the world would say, that if this dispensation could legalize the latter marriage, the former must have been legalized by it, and this would destroy the marriage of Anne Boleyn, and with it all Elizabeth's claims to the succession. She could not, then, marry Philip, without, by the very act, effectually undermining all her own rights to the throne. She was far too subtle and wary to stumble into such a pitfall as that.

Elizabeth rejected this and some other offers, and one or two years passed away. In the mean time, the people of the country, though they had no wish to have her marry such a stern and heartless tyrant as Philip of Spain, were very uneasy at the idea of her not being married at all. Her life would, of course, in due time, come to an end, and it was of immense importance to the peace and happiness of the realm that, after her death, there should be no doubt about the succession. If she were to be married and leave children, they would succeed to the throne without question; but if she were to die single and childless, the result would be, they feared, that the Catholics would espouse the cause of Mary Queen of Scots, and the Protestants that of some Protestant descendant of Henry VII., and thus the country be involved in all the horrors of a protracted civil war.

The House of Commons in those days was a very humble council, convened to discuss and settle mere internal and domestic affairs, and standing at a vast distance from the splendor and power of royalty, to which it looked up with the profoundest reverence and awe. The Commons, at the close of one of their sessions, ventured, in a very timid and cautious manner, to send a petition to the queen, urging her to consent, for the sake of the future peace of the realm, and the welfare of her subjects, to accept of a husband. Few single persons are offended at a recommendation of marriage, if properly offered, from whatever quarter it may come. The queen, in this instance, returned what was called a very gracious reply. She, however, very decidedly refused the request. She said that, as they had been very respectful in the form of their petition, and as they had confined it to general terms, without presuming to suggest either a person or a time, she would not take offense at their well-intended suggestion, but that she had no design of ever being married. At her coronation, she was married, she said, to her people, and the wedding ring was upon her finger still. Her people were the objects of all her affection and regard. She should never have any other spouse. She said she should be well contented to have it engraved upon her tomb-stone, "Here lies a queen who lived and died a virgin."

This answer silenced the Commons, but it did not settle the question in the public mind. Cases often occur of ladies saying very positively that they shall never consent to be married, and yet afterward altering their minds; and many ladies, knowing how frequently this takes place, sagaciously conclude that, whatever secret resolutions they may form, they will be silent about them, lest they get into a position from which it will be afterward awkward to retreat. The princes of the Continent and the nobles of England paid no regard to Elizabeth's declaration, but continued to do all in their power to obtain her hand.

One or two years afterward Elizabeth was attacked with the small-pox, and for a time was dangerously sick, in fact, for some days her life was despaired of, and the country was thrown into a great state of confusion and dismay. Parties began to form--the Catholics for Mary Queen of Scots, and the Protestants for the family of Jane Grey. Every thing portended a dreadful contest. Elizabeth, however, recovered; but the country had been so much alarmed at their narrow escape, that Parliament ventured once more to address the queen on the subject of her marriage. They begged that she would either consent to that measure, or, if she was finally determined not to do that, that she would cause a law to be passed, or an edict to be promulgated, deciding beforehand who was really to succeed to the throne in the event of her decease.

Elizabeth would not do either. Historians have speculated a great deal upon her motives; all that is certain is the fact, she would not do either.

But, though Elizabeth thus resisted all the plans formed for giving her a husband, she had, in her own court, a famous personal favorite, who has always been considered as in some sense her lover. His name was originally Robert Dudley, though she made him Earl of Leicester, and he is commonly designated in history by this latter name. He was a son of the Duke of

Northumberland, who was the leader of the plot for placing Lady Jane Grey upon the throne in the time of Mary. He was a very elegant and accomplished man, and young, though already married. Elizabeth advanced him to high offices and honors very early in her reign, and kept him much at court. She made him her Master of Horse, but she did not bestow upon him much real power. Cecil was her great counselor and minister of state. He was a cool, sagacious, wary man, entirely devoted to Elizabeth's interests, and to the glory and prosperity of the realm. He was at this time, as has already been stated, forty years of age, thirteen or fourteen years older than Elizabeth. Elizabeth showed great sagacity in selecting such a minister, and great wisdom in keeping him in power so long. He remained in her service all his life, and died at last, only a few years before Elizabeth, when he was nearly eighty years of age.

Dudley, on the other hand, was just about Elizabeth's own age. In fact, it is said by some of the chronicles of the times that he was born on the same day and hour with her. However this may be, he became a great personal favorite, and Elizabeth evinced a degree and kind of attachment to him which subjected her to a great deal of censure and reproach.

She could not be thinking of him for her husband, it would seem, for he was already married. Just about this time, however, a mysterious circumstance occurred, which produced a great deal of excitement, and has ever since marked a very important era in the history of Leicester and Elizabeth's attachment. It was the sudden and very singular death of Leicester's wife.

Leicester had, among his other estates, a lonely mansion in Berkshire, about fifty miles west of London. It was called Cumnor House. Leicester's wife was sent there, no one knew why; she went under the charge of a gentleman who was one of Leicester's dependents, and entirely devoted to his will. The house, too, was occupied by a man who had the character of being ready for any deed which might be required of him by his master. The name of Leicester's wife was Amy Robesart.

In a short time news came to London that the unhappy woman was killed by a fall down stairs! The instantaneous suspicion darted at once into every one's mind that she had been murdered. Rumors circulated all around the place where the death had occurred that she had been murdered. A conscientious clergyman of the neighborhood sent an account of the case to London, to the queen's ministers, stating the facts, and urging the queen to order an investigation of the affair, but nothing was ever done. It has accordingly been the general belief of mankind since that time, that the unprincipled courtier destroyed his wife in the vain hope of becoming afterward the husband of the queen.

The people of England were greatly incensed at this transaction. They had hated Leicester before, and they hated him now more inveterately still. Favorites are very generally hated; royal favorites always. He, however, grew more and more intimate with the queen, and every body feared that he was going to be her husband. Their conduct was watched very closely by all the great world, and, as is usual in such cases, a thousand circumstances and occurrences were reported busily from tongue to tongue, which the actors in them doubtless supposed passed unobserved or were forgotten.

One night, for instance, Queen Elizabeth, having supped with Dudley, was going home in her chair, lighted by torch-bearers. At the present day, all London is lighted brilliantly at midnight with gas, and ladies go home from their convivial and pleasure assemblies in luxurious carriages, in which they are rocked gently along through broad and magnificent avenues, as bright, almost, as day. Then, however, it was very different. The lady was borne slowly along through narrow, and dingy, and dangerous streets, with a train of torches before and behind her, dispelling the darkness a moment with their glare, and then leaving it more deep and somber than ever. On the night of which we are speaking, Elizabeth, feeling in good humor, began to talk with some of the torch-bearers on the way. They were Dudley's men, and Elizabeth began to praise their master. She said to one of them, among other things, that she was going to raise him to a higher position than any of his name had ever borne before. Now, as Dudley's father was a duke, which title denotes the highest rank of the English nobility, the man inferred that the queen's meaning was that she intended to marry him, and thus make him a sort of king. The man told the story boastingly to one of the servants of Lord Arundel, who was also a suitor of the queen's. The servants, each taking the part of his master in the rivalry, quarreled. Lord Arundel's man said that he wished that Dudley had been hung with his father, or else that somebody would shoot him in the street with a dag. A dag was, in the language of those days, the name for a pistol.

Time moved on, and though Leicester seemed to become more and more a favorite, the plan of his being married to Elizabeth, if any such were entertained by either party, appeared to come no nearer to an accomplishment. Elizabeth lived in great state and splendor, sometimes residing in her palaces in or near London, and sometimes making royal progresses about her dominions. Dudley, together with the other prominent members of her court, accompanied her on these excursions, and obviously enjoyed a very high degree of personal favor. She encouraged, at the same time, her other suitors, so that on all the great public occasions of state, at the tilts and tournaments, at the plays--which, by-the-way, in those days were performed in the churches-- on all the royal progresses and grand receptions at cities, castles, and universities, the lady queen was surrounded always by royal or noble beaux, who made her presents, and paid her a thousand compliments, and offered her gallant attentions without number--all prompted by ambition in the guise of love. They smiled upon the queen with a perpetual sycophancy, and gnashed their teeth secretly upon each other with a hatred which, unlike the pretended love, was at least honest and sincere. Leicester was the gayest, most accomplished, and most favored of them all, and the rest accordingly combined and agreed in hating him more than they did each other.

Queen Elizabeth, however, never really admitted that she had any design of making Leicester, or Dudley, as he is indiscriminately called, her husband. In fact, at one time she recommended him to Mary Queen of Scots for a husband. After Mary returned to Scotland, the two queens were, for a time, on good terms, as professed friends, though they were, in fact, all the time, most inveterate and implacable foes; but each, knowing how much injury the other might do her, wished to avoid exciting any unnecessary hostility. Mary, particularly, as she found she could not get possession of the English throne during Elizabeth's life-time, concluded to try to conciliate her, in hopes to persuade her to acknowledge, by act of Parliament, her right to the succession after her death. So she used to confer with Elizabeth on the subject of her own marriage, and to ask her advice about it. Elizabeth did not wish to have Mary married at all, and so she always proposed somebody who she knew would be out of the question. She at one time proposed Leicester, and for a time seemed quite in earnest about it, especially so long as Mary seemed averse to it. At length, however, when Mary, in order to test her sincerity, seemed inclined to yield, Elizabeth retreated in her turn, and withdrew her proposals. Mary then gave up the hope of satisfying Elizabeth in any way and married Lord Darnley without her consent.

Elizabeth's regard for Dudley, however, still continued. She made him Earl of Leicester, and granted him the magnificent castle of Kenilworth, with a large estate adjoining and surrounding it; the rents of the lands giving him a princely income, and enabling him to live in almost royal state. Queen Elizabeth visited him frequently in this castle. One of these visits is very minutely described by the chroniclers of the times. The earl made the most expensive and extraordinary preparations for the reception and entertainment of the queen and her retinue on this occasion. The moat--which is a broad canal filled with water surrounding the castle--had a floating island upon it, with a fictitious personage whom they called the lady of the lake upon the island, who sung a song in praise of Elizabeth as she passed the bridge. There was also an artificial dolphin swimming upon the water, with a band of musicians within it. As the queen advanced across the park, men and women, in strange disguises, came out to meet her, and to offer her salutations and praises. One was dressed as a sibyl, another like an American savage, and a third, who was concealed, represented an echo. This visit was continued for nineteen days, and the stories of the splendid entertainments provided for the company--the plays, the bear-baitings, the fireworks, the huntings, the mock fights, the feastings and revelries--filled all Europe at the time, and have been celebrated by historians and story-tellers ever since. The Castle of Kenilworth is now a very magnificent heap of ruins, and is explored every year by thousands of visitors from every quarter of the globe.

Leicester, if he ever really entertained any serious designs of being Elizabeth's husband at last gave up his hopes, and married another woman. This lady had been the wife of the Earl of Essex. Her husband died very suddenly and mysteriously just before Leicester married her. Leicester kept the marriage secret for some time, and when it came at last to the queen's knowledge she was exceedingly angry. She had him arrested and sent to prison. However, she gradually recovered from her fit of resentment, and by degrees restored him to her favor again.

Twenty years of Elizabeth's reign thus passed away, and no one of all her suitors had succeeded in obtaining her hand. All this time her government had been administered with much efficiency and power. All Europe had been in great commotion during almost the whole period, on account of the terrible conflicts which were raging between the Catholics and the Protestants, each party having been doing its utmost to exterminate and destroy the other. Elizabeth and her government took part, very frequently, in these contests; sometimes by negotiations, and sometimes by fleets and armies, but always sagaciously and cautiously, and generally with great effect. In the mean time, however, the queen, being now forty-five years of age, was rapidly approaching the time when questions of marriage could no longer be entertained. Her lovers, or, rather, her suitors, had, one after another, given up the pursuit, and disappeared from the field. One only seemed at length to remain, on the decision of whose fate the final result of the great question of the queen's marriage seemed to be pending.

It was the Duke of Anjou. He was a French prince. His brother, who had been the Duke of Anjou before him, was now King Henry III. of France. His own name was Francis. He was twenty five years younger than Elizabeth, and he was only seventeen years of age when it was first proposed that he should marry her. He was then Duke of Alenen. It was his mother's plan. She was the great Catharine de Medici, queen of France, and one of the most extraordinary women, for her talents, her management, and her power, that ever lived. Having one son upon the throne of France, she wanted the throne of England for the other. The negotiation had been pending fruitlessly for many years, and now, in 1581, it was vigorously renewed. The duke himself, who was at this time a young man of twenty-four or five, began to be impatient and earnest in his suit. There was, in fact, one good reason why he should be so. Elizabeth was forty-eight, and, unless the match were soon concluded, the time for effecting it would be obviously forever gone by.

He had never had an interview with the queen. He had seen pictures of her, however, and he sent an embassador over to England to urge his suit, and to convince Elizabeth how much he was in love with her charms. The name of this agent was Simier. He was a very polite and accomplished man, and soon learned the art of winning his way to Elizabeth's favor. Leicester was very jealous of his success. The two favorites soon imbibed a terrible enmity for each other. They filled the court with their quarrels. The progress of the negotiation, however, went on, the people taking sides very violently, some for and some against the projected marriage. The animosities became exceedingly virulent, until at length Simier's life seemed to be in danger. He said that Leicester had hired one of the guards to assassinate him; and it is a fact, that one day, as he and the queen, with other attendants, were making an excursion upon the river, a shot was fired from the shore into the barge. The shot did no injury except to wound one of the oarsmen, and frighten all the party pretty thoroughly. Some thought the shot was aimed at Simier, and others at the queen herself. It was afterward proved, or supposed to be proved, that this shot was the accidental discharge of a gun, without any evil intention whatever.

In the mean time, Elizabeth grew more and more interested in the idea of having the young duke for her husband; and it seemed as if the maidenly resolutions, which had stood their ground so firmly for twenty years, were to be conquered at last. The more, however, she seemed to approach toward a consent to the measure, the more did all the officers of her government, and the nation at large, oppose it. There were, in their minds, two insuperable objections to the match. The candidate was a Frenchman, and he was a papist.

The council interceded. Friends remonstrated. The nation murmured and threatened. A book was published entitled "The Discovery of a gaping Gulf wherein England is like to be swallowed up by another French marriage, unless the Lord forbid the Bans by letting her see the Sin and Punishment thereof." The author of it had his right hand cut off for his punishment.

At length, after a series of most extraordinary discussions, negotiations, and occurrences, which kept the whole country in a state of great excitement for a long time, the affair was at last all settled. The marriage articles, both political and personal, were all arranged. The nuptials were to be celebrated in six weeks. The duke came over in great state, and was received with all possible pomp and parade. Festivals and banquets were arranged without number, and in the most magnificent style, to do him and his attendants honor. At one of them, the queen took off a ring from her finger, and put it upon his, in the presence of a great assembly, which was the first announcement to the public that the affair was finally settled. The news spread every where with great rapidity. It produced in England great consternation and distress, but on the Continent it was welcomed with joy, and the great English alliance, now so obviously approaching, was celebrated with ringing of bells, bonfires, and grand illuminations.

And yet, notwithstanding all this, as soon as the obstacles were all removed, and there was no longer opposition to stimulate the determination of the queen, her heart failed her at last, and she finally concluded that she would not be married, after all. She sent for the duke one morning to come and see her. What takes place precisely between ladies and gentlemen when they break off their engagements is not generally very publicly known, but the duke came out from this interview in a fit of great vexation and anger. He pulled off the queen's ring and threw it from him, muttering curses upon the fickleness and faithlessness of women.

Still Elizabeth would not admit that the match was broken off. She continued to treat the duke with civility and to pay him many honors. He decided, however, to return to the Continent. She accompanied him a part of the way to the coast, and took leave of him with many professions of sorrow at the parting, and begged him to come back soon. This he promised to do, but he never returned. He lived some time afterward in comparative neglect and obscurity, and mankind considered the question of the marriage of Elizabeth as now, at last, settled forever.

CHAPTER IX.

PERSONAL CHARACTER.

1560-1586

Opinions of Elizabeth's character.--The Catholics and Protestants.--Parties in England.--Elizabeth's wise administration.--Mary claims the English throne.--She is made prisoner by Elizabeth.--Various plots.--Execution of Mary.--The impossibility of settling the claims of Mary and Elizabeth.--Elizabeth's duplicity.--Her scheming to entrap Mary.--Maiden ladies.--Their benevolent spirit.--Elizabeth's selfishness and jealousy.--The maids of honor.--Instance of Elizabeth's cruelty.--Her irritable temper.--Leicester's friend and the gentleman of the black rod.--Elizabeth in a rage.--Her invectives against Leicester.--Leicester's chagrin.--Elizabeth's powers of satire.--Elizabeth's views of marriage.--Her insulting conduct.--The Dean of Christ Church and the Prayer Book.--Elizabeth's good qualities.--Her courage.--The shot at the barge.--Elizabeth's vanity.--Elizabeth and the embassador.--The pictures.--Elizabeth's fondness for pomp and parade.--Summary of Elizabeth's character.

Mankind have always been very much divided in opinion in respect to the personal character of Queen Elizabeth, but in one point all have agreed, and that is, that in the management of public affairs she was a woman of extraordinary talent and sagacity, combining, in a very remarkable degree, a certain cautious good sense and prudence with the most determined resolution and energy.

She reigned about forty years, and during almost all that time the whole western part of the Continent of Europe was convulsed with the most terrible conflicts between the Protestant and Catholic parties. The predominance of power was with the Catholics, and was, of course, hostile to Elizabeth. She had, moreover, in the field a very prominent competitor for her throne in Mary Queen of Scots. The foreign Protestant powers were ready to aid this claimant, and there was, besides, in her own dominions a very powerful interest in her favor. The great divisions of sentiment in England, and the energy with which each party struggled against its opponents, produced, at all times, a prodigious pressure of opposing forces, which bore heavily upon the safety of the state and of Elizabeth's government, and threatened them with continual danger. The administration of public affairs moved on, during all this time, trembling continually under the heavy shocks it was constantly receiving, like a ship staggering on in a storm, its safety depending on the nice equilibrium between the shocks of the seas, the pressure of the wind upon the sails, and the weight and steadiness of the ballast below.

During all this forty years it is admitted that Elizabeth and her wise and sagacious ministers managed very admirably. They maintained the position and honor of England, as a Protestant power, with great success; and the country, during the whole period, made great progress in the arts, in commerce, and in improvements of every kind. Elizabeth's greatest danger, and her greatest source of solicitude during her whole reign, was from the claims of Mary Queen of Scots. We have already described the energetic measures which she took at the commencement of her reign to counter act and head off, at the outset, these dangerous pretensions. Though these efforts were triumphantly successful at the time, still the victory was not final. It postponed, but did not destroy, the danger. Mary continued to claim the English throne. Innumerable plots were beginning to be formed among the Catholics, in Elizabeth's own dominions, for making her queen. Foreign potentates and powers were watching an opportunity to assist in these plans. At last Mary, on account of internal difficulties in her own land, fled across the frontier into England to save her life, and Elizabeth made her prisoner.

In England, to plan or design the dethronement of a monarch is, in a subject, high treason. Mary had undoubtedly designed the dethronement of Elizabeth, and was waiting only an opportunity to accomplish it. Elizabeth, consequently, condemned her as guilty of treason, in effect; and Mary's sole defense against this charge was that she was not a subject. Elizabeth yielded to this plea, when she first found Mary in her power, so far as not to take her life, but she consigned her to a long and weary captivity.

This, however, only made the matter worse. It stimulated the enthusiasm and zeal of all the Catholics in England, to have their leader, and as they believed, their rightful queen, a captive in the midst of them, and they formed continually the most extensive and most dangerous plots. These plots were discovered and suppressed, one after another, each one producing more anxiety and alarm than the preceding. For a time Mary suffered no evil consequences from these discoveries further than an increase of the rigors of her confinement. At last the patience of the queen and of her government was exhausted. A law was passed against treason, expressed in such terms as to include Mary in the liability for its dreadful penalties although she was not a subject, in case of any new transgression; and when the next case occurred, they brought her to trial and condemned her to death. The sentence was executed in the gloomy castle of Fotheringay, where she was then confined.

As to the question whether Mary or Elizabeth had the rightful title to the English crown, it has not only never been settled, but from its very nature it can not be settled. It is one of those cases in which a peculiar contingency occurs which runs beyond the scope and reach of all the ordinary principles by which analogous cases are tried, and leads to questions which can not be decided. As long as a hereditary succession goes smoothly on, like a river keeping within its banks, we can decide subordinate and incidental questions which may arise; but when a case occurs in which we have the omnipotence of Parliament to set off against the infallibility of the pope--the sacred obligations of a will against the equally sacred principles of hereditary succession--and when we have, at last, two contradictory actions of the same ultimate umpire, we find all technical grounds of coming to a conclusion gone. We then, abandoning these, seek for some higher and more universal principles--

essential in the nature of things, and thus independent of the will and action of man--to see if they will throw any light on the subject. But we soon find ourselves as much perplexed and confounded in this inquiry as we were before. We ask, in beginning the investigation, What is the ground and nature of the right by which any king or queensucceeds to the power possessed by his ancestors? And we give up in despair, not being able to answer even this first preliminary inquiry.

Mankind have not, in their estimate of Elizabeth's character, condemned so decidedly the substantial acts which she performed, as the duplicity, the false-heartedness, and the false pretensions which she manifested in performing them. Had she said frankly and openly to Mary before the world, if these schemes for revolutionizing England and placing yourself upon the throne continue, your life must be forfeited, my own safety and the safety of the realm absolutely demand it; and then had fairly, and openly, and honestly executed her threat, mankind would have been silent on the subject, if they had not been satisfied. But if she had really acted thus, she would not have been Elizabeth. She, in fact, pursued a very different course. She maneuvered, schemed, and planned; she pretended to be full of the warmest affection for her cousin; she contrived plot after plot, and scheme after scheme, to ensnare her; and when, at last, the execution took place, in obedience to her own formal and written authority, she pretended to great astonishment and rage. She never meant that the sentence should take effect. She filled England, France, and Scotland with the loud expressions of her regret, and she punished the agents who had executed her will. This management was to prevent the friends of Mary from forming plans of revenge.

This was her character in all things. She was famous for her false pretensions and double dealings, and yet, with all her talents and sagacity, the disguise she assumed was sometimes so thin and transparent that her assuming it was simply ridiculous.

Maiden ladies, who spend their lives, in some respects, alone, often become deeply imbued with a kind and benevolent spirit, which seeks its gratification in relieving the pains and promoting the happiness of all around them. Conscious that the circumstances which have caused them to lead a single life would secure for them the sincere sympathy and the increased esteem of all who know them, if delicacy and propriety allowed them to be expressed, they feel a strong degree of self-respect, they live happily, and are a continual means of comfort and joy to all around them. This was not so, however, with Elizabeth. She was jealous, petulant, irritable. She envied others the love and the domestic enjoyments which ambition forbade her to share, and she seemed to take great pleasure in thwarting and interfering with the plans of others for securing this happiness.

One remarkable instance of this kind occurred. It seems she was sometimes accustomed to ask the young ladies of the court--her maids of honor--if they ever thought about being married, and they, being cunning enough to know what sort of an answer would please the queen always promptly denied that they did so. Oh no! they never thought about being married at all. There was one young lady, however, artless and sincere, who, when questioned in this way, answered, in her simplicity, that she often thought of it, and that she should like to be married very much, if her father would only consent to her union with a certain gentleman whom she loved. "Ah!" said Elizabeth; "well, I will speak to your father about it, and see what I can do." Not long after this the father of the young lady came to court, and the queen proposed the subject to him. The father said that he had not been aware that his daughter had formed such an attachment, but that he should certainly give his consent, without any hesitation, to any arrangement of that kind which the queen desired and advised. "That is all, then," said the queen; "I will do the rest." So she called the young lady into her presence, and told her that her father had given his free consent. The maiden's heart bounded with joy, and she began to express her happiness and her gratitude to the queen, promising to do every thing in her power to please her, when Elizabeth interrupted her, saying, "Yes, you will act so as to please me, I have no doubt, but you are not going to be a fool and get married. Your father has given his consent to me, and not to you, and you may rely upon it you will never get it out of my possession. You were pretty bold to acknowledge your foolishness to me so readily."

Elizabeth was very irritable, and could never bear any contradiction. In the case even of Leicester, who had such an unbounded influence over her, if he presumed a little too much he would meet sometimes a very severe rebuff, such as nobody but a courtier would endure; but courtiers, haughty and arrogant as they are in their bearing toward inferiors, are generally fawning sycophants toward those above them, and they will submit to any thing imaginable from a queen.

It was the custom in Elizabeth's days, as it is now among the great in European countries, to have a series or suite of rooms, one beyond the other, the inner one being the presence chamber, and the others being occupied by attendants and servants of various grades, to regulate and control the admission of company. Some of these officers were styled gentlemen of the black rod, that name being derived from a peculiar badge of authority which they were accustomed to carry. It happened, one day, that a certain gay captain, a follower of Leicester's, and a sort of favorite of his, was stopped in the antechamber by one of the gentlemen of the black rod, named Bowyer, the queen having ordered him to be more careful and particular in respect to the admission of company. The captain, who was proud of the favor which he enjoyed with Leicester, resented this affront, and threatened the officer, and he was engaged in an altercation with him on the subject when Leicester came in. Leicester took his favorite's part, and told the gentleman usher that he was a knave, and that he would have him turned out of office. Leicester was accustomed to feel so much confidence in his power over Elizabeth, that his manner toward all beneath him had become exceedingly haughty and overbearing. He supposed, probably, that the officer would humble himself at once before his rebukes.

The officer, however, instead of this, stepped directly in before Leicester, who was then going in himself to the presence of the queen; kneeled before her majesty, related the facts of the case, and humbly asked what it was her pleasure that he should do. He had obeyed her majesty's orders, he said, and had been called imperiously to account for it, and threatened violently by

Leicester, and he wished now to know whether Leicester was king or her majesty queen. Elizabeth was very much displeased with the conduct of her favorite. She turned to him, and, beginning with a sort of oath which she was accustomed to use when irritated and angry, she addressed him in invectives and reproaches the most severe. She gave him, in a word, what would be called a scolding, were it not that scolding is a term not sufficiently dignified for history, even for such humble history as this. She told him that she had indeed shown him favor, but her favor was not so fixed and settled upon him that nobody else was to have any share, and that if he imagined that he could lord it over her household, she would contrive a way very soon to convince him of his mistake. There was one mistress to rule there, she said, but no master. She then dismissed Bowyer, telling Leicester that, if any evil happened to him, she should hold him, that is, Leicester, to a strict account for it, as she should be convinced it would have come through his means.

Leicester was exceedingly chagrined at this result of the difficulty. Of course he dared not defend himself or reply. All the other courtiers enjoyed his confusion very highly, and one of them, in giving an account of the affair, said, in conclusion, that "the queen's words so quelled him, that, for some time after, his feigned humility was one of his best virtues."

Queen Elizabeth very evidently possessed that peculiar combination of quickness of intellect and readiness of tongue which enables those who possess it to say very sharp and biting things, when vexed or out of humor. It is a brilliant talent, though it always makes those who possess it hated and feared. Elizabeth was often wantonly cruel in the exercise of this satirical power, considering very little--as is usually the case with such persons--the justice of her invectives, but obeying blindly the impulses of the ill nature which prompted her to utter them. We have already said that she seemed always to have a special feeling of ill will against marriage and every thing that pertained to it, and she had, particularly, a theory that the bishops and the clergy ought not to be married. She could not absolutely prohibit their marrying, but she did issue an injunction forbidding any of the heads of the colleges or cathedrals to take their wives into the same, or any of their precincts. At one time, in one of her royal progresses through the country, she was received, and very magnificently and hospitably entertained, by the Archbishop of Canterbury, at his palace. The archbishop's wife exerted herself very particularly to please the queen and to do her honor. Elizabeth evinced her gratitude by turning to her, as she was about to take her leave, and saying that she could not call her the archbishop's wife, and did not like to call her his mistress, and so she did not know what to call her; but that, at all events, she was very much obliged to her for her hospitality.

Elizabeth's highest officers of state were continually exposed to her sharp and sudden reproaches, and they often incurred them by sincere and honest efforts to gratify and serve her. She had made an arrangement, one day, to go into the city of London to St. Paul's Church, to hear the Dean of Christ Church, a distinguished clergyman, preach. The dean procured a copy of the Prayer Book, and had it splendidly bound, with a great number of beautiful and costly prints interleaved in it. These prints were all of a religious character, being representations of sacred history, or of scenes in the lives of the saints. The volume, thus prepared, was very beautiful, and it was placed, when the Sabbath morning arrived, upon the queen's cushion at the church, ready for her use. The queen entered in great state, and took her seat in the midst of all the parade and ceremony customary on such occasions. As soon, however, as she opened the book and saw the pictures, she frowned, and seemed to be much displeased. She shut the book and put it away, and called for her own; and, after the service, she sent for the dean, and asked him who brought that book there. He replied, in a very humble and submissive manner, that he had procured it himself, having intended it as a present for her majesty. This only produced fresh expressions of displeasure. She proceeded to rebuke him severely for countenancing such a popish practice as the introduction of pictures in the churches. All this time Elizabeth had herself a crucifix in her own private chapel, and the dean himself, on the other hand, was a firm and consistent Protestant, entirely opposed to the Catholic system of images and pictures, as Elizabeth very well knew.

This sort of roughness was a somewhat masculine trait of character for a lady, it must be acknowledged, and not a very agreeable one, even in man; but with some of the bad qualities of the other sex, Elizabeth possessed, also, some that were good. She was courageous, and she evinced her courage sometimes in a very noble manner. At one time, when political excitement ran very high, her friends thought that there was serious danger in her appearing openly in public, and they urged her not to do it, but to confine herself within her palaces for a time, until the excitement should pass away. But no; the representations made to her produced no effect. She said she would continue to go out just as freely as ever. She did not think that there was really any danger; and besides, if there was, she did not care; she would rather take her chance of being killed than to be kept shut up like a prisoner.

At the time, too, when the shot was fired at the barge in which she was going down the Thames, many of her ministers thought it was aimed at her. They endeavored to convince her of this, and urged her not to expose herself to such dangers. She replied that she did not believe that the shot was aimed at her; and that, in fact, she would not believe any thing of her subjects which a father would not be willing to believe of his own children. So she went on sailing in her barge just as before.

Elizabeth was very vain of her beauty, though, unfortunately, she had very little beauty to be vain of. Nothing pleased her so much as compliments. She sometimes almost exacted them. At one time, when a distinguished embassador from Mary Queen of Scots was at her court, she insisted on his telling her whether she or Mary was the most beautiful. When we consider that Elizabeth was at this time over thirty years of age, and Mary only twenty-two, and that the fame of Mary's loveliness had filled the world, it must be admitted that this question indicated a considerable degree of self-complacency. The embassador had the prudence to attempt to evade the inquiry. He said at first that they were both beautiful enough. But Elizabeth wanted to know, she said, which was most beautiful. The embassador then said that his queen was the most beautiful queen in Scotland and Elizabeth in England. Elizabeth was not satisfied with this, but insisted on a definite answer to her question; and the embassador said at last that Elizabeth had the fairest complexion, though Mary was considered a very lovely woman. Elizabeth then wanted to know which was the tallest of the two. The embassador said that Mary was. "Then," said Elizabeth, "she is too tall, for I am just of the right height myself."

At one time during Elizabeth's reign, the people took a fancy to engrave and print portraits of her, which, being perhaps tolerably faithful to the original, were not very alluring. The queen was much vexed at the circulation of these prints, and finally she caused a grave and formal proclamation to be issued against them. In this proclamation it was stated that it was the intention of the queen, at some future time, to have a proper artist employed to execute a correct and true portrait of herself, which should then be published; and, in the mean time, all persons were forbidden to make or sell any representations of her whatever.

Elizabeth was extremely fond of pomp and parade. The magnificence and splendor of the celebrations and festivities which characterized her reign have scarcely ever been surpassed in any country or in any age. She once went to attend Church, on a particular occasion, accompanied by a thousand men in full armor of steel, and ten pieces of cannon, with drums and trumpets sounding. She received her foreign embassadors with military spectacles and shows, and with banquets and parties of pleasure, which for many days kept all London in a fever of excitement. Sometimes she made excursions on the river, with whole fleets of boats and barges in her train; the shores, on such occasions, swarming with spectators, and waving with flags and banners. Sometimes she would make grand progresses through her dominions, followed by an army of attendants--lords and ladies dressed and mounted in the most costly manner--and putting the nobles whose seats she visited to a vast expense in entertaining such a crowd of visitors. Being very saving of her own means, she generally contrived to bring the expense of this magnificence upon others. The honor was a sufficient equivalent. Or, if it was not, nobody dared to complain.

To sum up all, Elizabeth was very great, and she was, at the same time, very little. Littleness and greatness mingled in her character in a manner which has scarcely ever been paralleled, except by the equally singular mixture of admiration and contempt with which mankind have always regarded her.

CHAPTER X.

THE INVINCIBLE ARMADA.

1585-1588

Fierce contests between Catholics and Protestants.--Philip's cruelty.--Effects of war.--Napoleon and Xerxes.--March of improvement.--Spanish armadas.--The Low Countries.--Their situation and condition.--Embassage from the Low Countries.--Their proposition.--Elizabeth's decision.--Leicester and Drake.--Leicester sets out for the Low Countries.--His reception.--Leicester's elation.--Elizabeth's displeasure.--Drake's success.--His deeds of cruelty.--Drake's expedition in 1577.--Execution of Doughty.--Straits of Magellan.--Drake plunders the Spaniards.--Chase of the Cacofogo.--Drake captures her.--Drake's escape by going round the world.--Character of Drake.--Philip demands the treasure.--Alarming news.--Elizabeth's navy.--Drake's expedition against the Spaniards.--His bold stroke.--Exasperation of Philip.--His preparations.--Elizabeth's preparations.--The army and navy.--Elizabeth reviews the troops.--Her speech.--Elizabeth's energy.--Approach of the armada.--A grand spectacle.--A singular fight.--Defeat of the armada.--A remnant escapes.

Thirty years of Queen Elizabeth's reign passed away. During all this time the murderous contests between the Catholic governments of France and Spain and their Protestant subjects went on with terrible energy. Philip of Spain was the great leader and head of the Catholic powers, and he prosecuted his work of exterminating heresy with the sternest and most merciless determination. Obstinate and protracted wars, cruel tortures, and imprisonments and executions without number, marked his reign.

Notwithstanding all this, however, strange as it may seem, the country increased in population, wealth, and prosperity. It is, after all, but a very small proportion of fifty millions of people which the most cruel monster of a tyrant can kill, even if he devotes himself fully to the work. The natural deaths among the vast population within the reach of Philip's power amounted, probably, to two millions every year; and if he destroyed ten thousand every year, it was only adding one death by violence to two hundred produced by accidents, disasters, or age. Dreadful as are the atrocities of persecution and war, and vast and incalculable as are the encroachments on human happiness which they produce, we are often led to overrate their relative importance, compared with the aggregate value of the interests and pursuits which are left unharmed by them, by not sufficiently appreciating the enormous extent and magnitude of these interests and pursuits in such communities as England, France, and Spain.

Sometimes, it is true, the operations of military heroes have been on such a prodigious scale as to make very serious inroads on the population of the greatest states. Napoleon for instance, on one occasion took five hundred thousand men out of France for his expedition to Russia. The campaign destroyed nearly all of them. It was only a very insignificant fraction of the vast army that ever returned. By this transaction, Napoleon thus just about doubled the annual mortality in France at a single blow. Xerxes enjoys the glory of having destroyed about a million of men--and these, not enemies, but countrymen, followers, and friends--in the same way, on a single expedition. Such vast results, however, were not attained in the conflicts which marked the reigns of Elizabeth and Philip of Spain. Notwithstanding the long-protracted international wars, and dreadful civil commotions of the period, the world went on increasing in wealth and population, and all the arts and improvements of life made very rapid progress. America had been discovered, and the way to the East Indies had been opened to European ships, and the Spaniards, the Portuguese, the Dutch, the English, and the French, had fleets of merchant vessels and ships of war in every sea. The Spaniards, particularly, had acquired great possessions in America, which contained very rich mines of gold and silver, and there was a particular kind of vessels called galleons, which went regularly once a year, under a strong convoy, to bring home the treasure. They used to call these fleets armada, which is the Spanish word denoting an armed squadron. Nations at war with Spain always made great efforts to intercept and seize these ships on their homeward voyages, when, being laden with gold and silver, they became prizes of the highest value.

Things were in this state about the year 1585, when Queen Elizabeth received a proposition from the Continent of Europe which threw her into great perplexity. Among the other dominions of Philip of Spain, there were certain states situated in the broad tract of low, level land which lies northeast of France, and which constitutes, at the present day, the countries of Holland and Belgium. This territory was then divided into several provinces, which were called, usually, the Low Countries, on account of the low and level situation of the land. In fact, there are vast tracts of land bordering the shore, which lie so low that dikes have to be built to keep out the sea. In these cases, there are lines of windmills, of great size and power, all along the coast, whose vast wings are always slowly revolving, to pump out the water which percolates through the dikes, or which flows from the water-courses after showers of rain.

The Low Countries were very unwilling to submit to the tyrannical government which Philip exercised over them. The inhabitants were generally Protestants, and Philip persecuted them cruelly. They were, in consequence of this, continually rebelling against his authority, and Elizabeth secretly aided them in these struggles, though she would not openly assist them, as she did not wish to provoke Philip to open war. She wished them success, however, for she knew very well that if Philip could once subdue his Protestant subjects at home, he would immediately turn his attention to England, and perhaps undertake to depose Elizabeth, and place some Catholic prince or princess upon the throne in her stead.

Things were in this state in 1585, when the confederate provinces of the Low Countries sent an embassage to Elizabeth, offering her the government of the country as sovereign queen, if she would openly espouse their cause and protect them from Philip's power. This proposition called for very serious and anxious consideration. Elizabeth felt very desirous to make this addition to her dominions on its own account, and besides, she saw at once that such an acquisition would give her a great advantage in her future contests with Philip, if actual war must come. But then, on the other hand, by accepting the proposition, war must necessarily be brought on at once. Philip would, in fact, consider her espousing the cause of his rebellious subjects as an actual declaration of war on her part, so that making such a league with these countries would plunge her at once into hostilities with the greatest and most extended power on the globe. Elizabeth was very unwilling thus to precipitate the contest; but then, on the other hand, she wished very much to avoid the danger that threatened, of Philip's first subduing his own dominions, and then advancing to the invasion of England with his undivided strength. She finally concluded not to accept the sovereignty of the countries, but to make a league, offensive and defensive, with the governments, and to send out a fleet and an army to aid them. This, as she had expected, brought on a general war.

The queen commissioned Leicester to take command of the forces which were to proceed to Holland and the Netherlands; she also equipped a fleet, and placed it under the command of Sir Francis Drake, a very celebrated naval captain, to proceed across the Atlantic and attack the Spanish possessions on the American shores. Leicester was extremely elated with his appointment, and set off on his expedition with great pomp and parade. He had not generally, during his life, held stations of any great trust or responsibility. The queen had conferred upon him high titles and vast estates, but she had confided all real power to far more capable and trustworthy hands. She thought however, perhaps, that Leicester would answer for her allies; so she gave him his commission and sent him forth, charging him, with many injunctions, as he went away, to be discreet and faithful, and to do nothing which should compromise, in any way, her interests or honor.

It will, perhaps, be recollected that Leicester's wife had been, before her marriage with him, the wife of a nobleman named the Earl of Essex. She had a son, who, at his father's death, succeeded to the title. This young Essex accompanied Leicester on this occasion. His subsequent adventures, which were romantic and extraordinary, will be narrated in the next chapter.

The people of the Netherlands, being extremely desirous to please Elizabeth, their new ally, thought that they could not honor the great general she had sent them too highly. They received him with most magnificent military parades, and passed a vote in their assembly investing him with absolute authority as head of the government, thus putting him, in fact, in the very position which Elizabeth had herself declined receiving. Leicester was extremely pleased and elated with these honors. He was king all but in name. He provided himself with a noble life-guard, in imitation of royalty, and assumed all the state and airs of a monarch. Things went on so very prosperously with him for a short time, until he was one day thunderstruck by the appearance at his palace of a nobleman from the queen's court, named Heneage, who brought him a letter from Elizabeth which was in substance as follows:

"How foolishly, and with what contempt of my authority, I think you have acted, the messenger I now send to you will explain. I little imagined that a man whom I had raised from the dust, and treated with so much favor, would have forgotten all his obligations, and acted in such a manner. I command you now to put yourself entirely under the direction of this messenger, to do in all things precisely as he requires, upon pain of further peril."

Leicester humbled himself immediately under this rebuke, sent home most ample apologies and prayers for forgiveness, and, after a time, gradually recovered the favor of the queen. He soon, however, became very unpopular in the Netherlands. Grievous complaints were made against him, and he was at length recalled.

Drake was more successful. He was a bold, undaunted, and energetic seaman, but unprincipled and merciless. He manned and equipped his fleet, and set sail toward the Spanish possessions in America. He attacked the colonies, sacked the towns, plundered the inhabitants, intercepted the ships, and searched them for silver and gold. In a word, he did exactly what pirates are hung for doing, and execrated afterward by all mankind. But, as Queen Elizabeth gave him permission to perform these exploits, he has always been applauded by mankind as a hero. We would not be understood as denying that there is any difference between burning and plundering innocent towns and robbing ships, whether there is or is not a governmental permission to commit these crimes. There certainly is a difference. It only seems to us surprising that there should be so great a difference as is made by the general estimation of mankind.

Drake, in fact, had acquired a great and honorable celebrity for such deeds before this time, by a similar expedition, several years before, in which he had been driven to make the circumnavigation of the globe. England and Spain were then nominally at peace, and the expedition was really in pursuit of prizes and plunder.

Drake took five vessels with him on this his first expedition, but they were all very small. The largest was only a vessel of one hundred tons, while the ships which are now built are often of three thousand. With this little fleet Drake set sail boldly, and crossed the Atlantic, being fifty-five days out of sight of land. He arrived at last on the coast of South America, and then turned his course southward, toward the Straits of Magellan. Two of his vessels, he found, were so small as to be of very little service; so he shipped the men on board the others, and turned the two adrift. When he got well into the southern seas, he charged his chief mate, whose name was Doughty, with some offense against the discipline of his little fleet, and had him condemned to death. He was executed at the Straits of Magellan--beheaded. Before he died, the unhappy convict had the sacrament administered to him, Drake himself partaking of it with him. It was said, and believed at the time, that the charge against Doughty was only a pretense, and that the real cause of his death was that Leicester had agreed with Drake to kill him when far away, on account of his having assisted, with others, in spreading the reports that Leicester had murdered the Earl of Essex, the former husband of his wife.

The little squadron passed through the Straits of Magellan, and then encountered a dreadful storm, which separated the ships, and drove them several hundred miles to the westward, over the then boundless and trackless waters of the Pacific Ocean. Drake himself afterward recovered the shore with his own ship alone, and moved northward. He found Spanish ships and

Spanish merchants every where, who, not dreaming of the presence of an English enemy in those distant seas, were entirely secure; and they fell, one after another, a very easy prey. The very extraordinary story is told of his finding, in one place, a Spaniard asleep upon the shore, waiting, perhaps, for a boat, with thirty bars of silver by his side, of great weight and value, which Drake and his men seized and carried off, without so much as waking the owner. In one harbor which he entered he found three ships, from which the seamen had all gone ashore, leaving the vessels completely unguarded, so entirely unconscious were they of any danger near. Drake broke into the cabins of these ships, and found fifty or sixty wedges of pure silver there, of twenty pounds each. In this way, as he passed along the coast, he collected an immense treasure in silver and gold, both coin and bullion, without having to strike a blow for it. At last he heard of a very rich ship, called the Cacofogo, which had recently sailed for Panama, to which place they were taking the treasure, in order that it might be transported across the isthmus, and so taken home to Spain; for, before Drake's voyage, scarcely a single vessel had ever passed round Cape Horn. The ships which he had plundered had been all built upon the coast, by Spaniards who had come across the country at the Isthmus of Darien, and were to be used only to transport the treasure northward, where it could be taken across to the Gulf of Mexico.

Drake gave chase to the Cacofogo. At last he came near enough to fire into her, and one of his first shots cut away her foremast and disabled her. He soon captured the ship, and he found immense riches on board. Besides pearls and precious stones of great value, there were eighty pounds of gold, thirteen chests of silver coin, and silver enough in bars "to ballast a ship."

Drake's vessel was now richly laden with treasures, but in the mean time the news of his plunderings had gone across the Continent, and some Spanish ships of war had gone south to intercept him at the Straits of Magellan on his return. In this dilemma, the adventurous sailor conceived of the sublime idea of avoiding them by going round the world to get home. He pushed boldly forward, therefore, across the Pacific Ocean to the East Indies, thence through the Indian Ocean to the Cape of Good Hope, and, after three years from the time he left England, he returned to it safely again, his ship loaded with the plundered silver and gold.

As soon as he arrived in the Thames, the whole world flocked to see the little ship that had performed all these wonders. The vessel was drawn up alongside the land, and a bridge made to it, and, after the treasure was taken out, it was given up, for some time, to banquetings and celebrations of every kind. The queen took possession of all the treasure, saying that Philip might demand it, and she be forced to make restitution, for it must be remembered that all this took place several years before the war. She, however, treated the successful sailor with every mark of consideration and honor; she went herself on board his ship, and partook of an entertainment there, conferring the honor of knighthood, at the same time, on the admiral, so that "Sir Francis Drake" was thenceforth his proper title.

If the facts already stated do not give sufficient indications of the kind of character which in those days made a naval hero, one other circumstance may be added. At one time during this voyage, a Spaniard, whose ship Drake had spared, made him a present of a beautiful negro girl. Drake kept her on board his ship for a time, and then sent her ashore on some island that he was passing, and inhumanly abandoned her there, to become a mother among strangers, utterly friendless and alone. It must be added, however, in justice to the rude men among whom this wild buccaneer lived, that, though they praised all his other deeds of violence and wrong, this atrocious cruelty was condemned. It had the effect, even in those days, of tarnishing his fame.

Philip did claim the money, but Elizabeth found plenty of good excuses for not paying it over to him.

This celebrated expedition occupied more than three years. Going round the world is a long journey. The arrival of the ship in London took place in 1581, four years before the war actually broke out between England and Spain, which was in 1585; and it was in consequence of the great celebrity which Drake had acquired in this and similar excursions, that when at last hostilities commenced, he was put in command of the naval preparations. It was not long before it was found that his services were likely to be required near home, for rumors began to find their way to England that Philip was preparing a great fleet for the actual invasion of England. The news put the whole country into a state of great alarm.

The reader, in order to understand fully the grounds for this alarm, must remember that in those days Spain was the mistress of the ocean, and not England herself. Spain possessed the distant colonies and the foreign commerce, and built and armed the great ships, while England had comparatively few ships, and those which she had were small. To meet the formidable preparations which the Spaniards were making, Elizabeth equipped only four ships. To these however, the merchants of London added twenty or thirty more, of various sizes, which they furnished on condition of having a share in the plunder which they hoped would be secured. The whole fleet was put under Drake's command.

Robbers and murderers, whether those that operate upon the sea or on the land, are generally courageous, and Drake's former success had made him feel doubly confident and strong. Philip had collected a considerable fleet of ships in Cadiz, which is a strong sea-port in the southeastern part of Spain, on the Mediterranean Sea, and others were assembling in all the ports and bays along the shore, wherever they could be built or purchased. They were to rendezvous finally at Cadiz. Drake pushed boldly forward, and, to the astonishment of the world, forced his way into the harbor, through a squadron of galleys stationed there to protect the entrance, and burned, sunk, and destroyed more than a hundred ships which had been collected there. The whole work was done, and the little English fleet was off again, before the Spaniards could recover from their astonishment. Drake then sailed along the coast, seizing and destroying all the ships he could find. He next pushed to sea a little way, and had the good fortune to intercept and capture a richly-laden ship of very large size, called a carrack, which was coming home from the East Indies. He then went back to England in triumph. He said he had been "singeing the whiskers" of the King of Spain.

The booty was divided among the London merchants, as had been agreed upon. Philip was exasperated and enraged beyond expression at this unexpected destruction of armaments which had cost him so much time and money to prepare. His spirit was irritated and aroused by the disaster, not quelled; and he immediately began to renew his preparations, making them now on a still vaster scale than before. The amount of damage which Drake effected was, therefore, after all, of no greater benefit to England than putting back the invasion for about a year.

At length, in the summer of 1588, the preparations for the sailing of the great armada, which was to dethrone Elizabeth and bring back the English nation again under the dominion of some papal prince, and put down, finally, the cause of Protestantism in Europe, were complete. Elizabeth herself, and the English people, in the mean time, had not been idle. The whole kingdom had been for months filled with enthusiasm to prepare for meeting the foe. Armies were levied and fleets raised. Every maritime town furnished ships; and rich noblemen, in many cases, built or purchased vessels with their own funds, and sent them forward ready for the battle, as their contribution toward the means of defense. A large part of the force thus raised was stationed at Plymouth, which is the first great sea-port which presents itself on the English coast in sailing up the Channel. The remainder of it was stationed at the other end of the Channel, near the Straits of Dover, for it was feared that, in addition to the vast armament which Philip was to bring from Spain, he would raise another fleet in the Netherlands, which would, of course, approach the shores of England from the German Ocean.

Besides the fleets, a large army was raised. Twenty thousand men were distributed along the southern shores of England in such positions as to be most easily concentrated at any point where the armada might attempt to land and about as many more were marched down the Thames, and encamped near the mouth of the river, to guard that access. This encampment was at a place on the northern bank of the river, just above its mouth. Leicester, strange as it may seem, was put in command of this army. The queen, however, herself, went to visit this encampment, and reviewed the troops in person. She rode to and fro on horseback along the lines, armed like a warrior. At least she had a corslet of polished steel over her magnificent dress, and bore a general's truncheon, a richly-ornamented staff used as a badge of command. She had a helmet, too, with a white plume. This, however she did not wear. A page bore it, following her, while she rode, attended by Leicester and the other generals, all mounted on horses and splendidly caparisoned, from rank to rank, animating the men to the highest enthusiasm by her courageous bearing, her look of confidence, and her smiles.

She made an address to the soldiers. She said that she had been warned by some of her ministers of the danger of trusting herself to the power of such an armed multitude, for these forces were not regularly enlisted troops, but volunteers from among the citizens, who had suddenly left the ordinary avocations and pursuits of life to defend their country in this emergency. She had, however, she said, no such apprehensions of danger. She could trust herself without fear to the courage and fidelity of her subjects, as she had always, during all her reign, considered her greatest strength and safeguard as consisting in their loyalty and good will. For herself, she had come to the camp, she assured them, not for the sake of empty pageantry and parade, but to take her share with them in the dangers, and toils, and terrors of the actual battle. If Philip should land, they would find their queen in the hottest of the conflict, fighting by their sides. "I have," said she, "I know, only the body of a weak and feeble woman, but I have the heart of a king; and I am ready for my God, my kingdom, and my people, to have that body laid down, even in the dust. If the battle comes, therefore, I shall myself be in the midst and front of it, to live or die with you."

These were, thus far, but words, it is true, and how far Elizabeth would have vindicated their sincerity, if the entrance of the armada into the Thames had put her to the test, we can not now know. Sir Francis Drake saved her from the trial. One morning a small vessel came into the harbor at Plymouth, where the English fleet was lying, with the news that the armada was coming up the Channel under full sail. The anchors of the fleet were immediately raised, and great exertions made to get it out of the harbor, which was difficult, as the wind at the time was blowing directly in. The squadron got out at last, as night was coming on. The next morning the armada hove in sight, advancing from the westward up the Channel, in a vast crescent, which extended for seven miles from north to south, and seemed to sweep the whole sea.

It was a magnificent spectacle, and it was the ushering in of that far grander spectacle still, of which the English Channel was the scene for the ten days which followed, during which the enormous naval structures of the armada, as they slowly made their way along, were followed, and fired upon, and harassed by the smaller, and lighter, and more active vessels of their English foes. The unwieldy monsters pressed on, surrounded and worried by their nimbler enemies like hawks driven by kingfishers through the sky. Day after day this most extraordinary contest, half flight and half battle continued, every promontory on the shores covered all the time with spectators, who listened to the distant booming of the guns, and watched the smokes which arose from the cannonading and the conflagrations. One great galleon after another fell a prey. Some were burned, some taken as prizes, some driven ashore; and finally, one dark night, the English sent a fleet of fire-ships, all in flames, into the midst of the anchorage to which the Spaniards had retired, which scattered them in terror and dismay, and completed the discomfiture of the squadron.

The result was, that by the time the invincible armada had made its way through the Channel, and had passed the Straits of Dover, it was so dispersed, and shattered, and broken, that its commanders, far from feeling any disposition to sail up the Thames, were only anxious to make good their escape from their indefatigable and tormenting foes. They did not dare, in attempting to make this escape, to return through the Channel, so they pushed northward into the German Ocean. Their only course for getting back to Spain again was to pass round the northern side of England, among the cold and stormy seas that are rolling in continually among the ragged rocks and gloomy islands which darken the ocean there. At last a miserable remnant of the fleet--less than half--made their way back to Spain again.

CHAPTER XI.

THE EARL OF ESSEX.

1588-1600

Character of Essex.--Death of Leicester.--Essex becomes the queen's favorite.--Cecil and Essex.--Elizabeth's regard for Essex.--His impulsive bravery.--Essex's ardor for battle.--His duel.--Elizabeth's remark upon the duel.--She gives Essex a ring.--The quarrel.--The box on the ear.--Mortification of Essex.--He and Elizabeth reconciled.--Essex sent to Ireland.--Curious negotiations.--The queen's displeasure.--Essex's sudden return.--Essex is arrested.--Resentment and love.--Essex's anger and chagrin.--He is taken sick.--Nature of Essex's sickness.--The queen's anxiety.--The queen's kindness to Essex.--They are reconciled again.--Essex's promises.--The queen's ungenerous conduct.--Essex's monopoly of wines.--The queen refuses to renew it.--Essex made desperate.--His treasonable schemes.--Ramifications of the plot.--It is discovered.--Anxious deliberations.--The rising determined upon.--The hostages.--Essex enters the city.--The proclamation.--Essex unsuccessful.--Essex's hopeless condition.--He escapes to his palace.--Essex made prisoner, tried, and condemned.--His remorse.--Elizabeth's distress.--The ring not sent.--The warrant signed.--The platform.--Essex's last words.--The closing scene.--The courtier.--His fiendish pleasure.

The lady whom the Earl of Leicester married was, a short time before he married her, the wife of the Earl of Essex, and she had one son, who, on the death of his father, became the Earl of Essex in his turn. He came to court, and continued in Leicester's family after his mother's second marriage. He was an accomplished and elegant young man, and was regarded with a good deal of favor by the queen. He was introduced at court when he was but seventeen years old, and, being the step-son of Leicester, he necessarily occupied a conspicuous position; his personal qualities, joined with this, soon gave him a very high and honorable name.

About a month after the victory obtained by the English over the invincible armada, Leicester was seized with a fever on a journey, and, after lingering for a few days, died, leaving Essex, as it were, in his place. Elizabeth seems not to have been very inconsolable for her favorite's death. She directed, or allowed, his property to be sold at auction, to pay some debts which he owed her--or, as the historians of the day express it, which he owed the crown--and then seemed at once to transfer her fondness and affection to the young Essex, who was at that time twenty-one years of age. Elizabeth herself was now nearly sixty. Cecil was growing old also, and was somewhat infirm, though he had a son who was rapidly coming forward in rank and influence at court. This son's name was Robert. The young Earl of Essex's name was Robert too. The elder Cecil and Leicester had been, all their lives, watchful and jealous of each other, and in some sense rivals. Robert Cecil and Robert Devereux--for that was, in full, the Earl of Essex's family name--being young and ardent, inherited the animosity of their parents, and were less cautious and wary in expressing it. They soon became open foes.

Robert Devereux, or Essex, as he is commonly called in history, was handsome and accomplished, ardent, impulsive, and generous. The war with Spain, notwithstanding the destruction of the armada, continued, and Essex entered into it with all zeal. The queen, who with all her ambition, and her proud and domineering spirit, felt, like any other woman, the necessity of having something to love, soon began to take a strong interest in his person and fortunes, and seemed to love him as a mother loves a son; and he, in his turn, soon learned to act toward her as a son, full of youthful courage and ardor, often acts toward a mother over whose heart he feels that he has a strong control. He would go away, without leave, to mix in affrays with the Spanish ships in the English Channel and in the Bay of Biscay, and then come back and make his peace with the queen by very humble petitions for pardon, and promises of future obedience. When he went, with her leave, on these expeditions, she would charge his superior officers to keep him out of danger; while he, with an impetuosity which strongly marked his character, would evade and escape from all these injunctions, and press forward into every possible exposure, always eager to have battle given, and to get, himself, into the hottest part of it, when it was begun. At one time, off Cadiz, the officers of the English ships hesitated some time whether to venture an attack upon some ships in the harbor--Essex burning with impatience all the time--and when it was at length decided to make the attack, he was so excited with enthusiasm and pleasure that he threw his cap up into the air, and overboard, perfectly wild with delight, like a school-boy in anticipation of a holiday.

Ten years passed away, and Essex rose higher and higher in estimation and honor. He was sometimes in the queen's palaces at home, and sometimes away on the Spanish seas, where he acquired great fame. He was proud and imperious at court, relying on his influence with the queen, who treated him as a fond mother treats a spoiled child. She was often vexed with his conduct, but she could not help loving him. One day, as he was coming into the queen's presence chamber, he saw one of the courtiers there who had a golden ornament upon his arm which the queen had given him the day before. He asked what it was; they told him it was a "favor" from the queen. "Ah," said he, "I see how it is going to be; every fool must have his favor." The courtier resented this mode of speaking of his distinction, and challenged Essex to a duel. The combatants met in the Park, and Essex was disarmed and wounded. The queen heard of the affair, and, after inquiring very curiously about all the particulars, she said that she was glad of it; for, unless there was somebody to take down his pride, there would be no such thing as doing any thing with him.

Elizabeth's feelings toward Essex fluctuated in strange alternations of fondness and displeasure. At one time, when affection was in the ascendency, she gave him a ring, as a talisman of her protection. She promised him that if he ever should become involved in troubles or difficulties of any kind, and especially if he should lose her favor, either by his own misconduct or by the false accusations of his enemies, if he would send her that ring, it should serve to recall her former kind regard, and incline her to pardon and save him. Essex took the ring, and preserved it with the utmost care.

Friendship between persons of such impetuous and excitable temperaments as Elizabeth and Essex both possessed, though usually very ardent for a time, is very precarious and uncertain in duration. After various petulant and brief disputes, which were easily reconciled, there came at length a serious quarrel. There was, at that time, great difficulty in Ireland; a rebellion had broken out, in fact, which was fomented and encouraged by Spanish influence. Essex was one day urging very strongly the appointment of one of his friends to take the command there, while the queen was disposed to appoint another person. Essex urged his views and wishes with much importunity, and when he found that the queen was determined not to yield, he turned his back upon her in a contemptuous and angry manner. The queen lost patience in her turn, and, advancing rapidly to him, her eyes sparkling with extreme resentment and displeasure, she gave him a severe box on the ear, telling him, at the same time, to "go and be hanged." Essex was exceedingly enraged; he clasped the handle of his sword, but was immediately seized by the other courtiers present. They, however, soon released their hold upon him, and he walked off out of the apartment, saying that he could not and would not bear such an insult as that. He would not have endured it, he said, from King Henry the Eighth himself. The name of King Henry the Eighth, in those days, was the symbol and personification of the highest possible human grandeur.

The friends of Essex among the courtiers endeavored to soothe and calm him, and to persuade him to apologize to the queen, and seek a reconciliation. They told him that, whether right or wrong, he ought to yield; for in contests with the law or with a prince, a man, they said, ought, if wrong, to submit himself to justice; if right, to necessity; in either case, it was his duty to submit.

This was very good philosophy; but Essex was not in a state of mind to listen to philosophy. He wrote a reply to the friend who had counseled him as above, that "the queen had the temper of a flint; that she had treated him with such extreme injustice and cruelty so many times that his patience was exhausted, and he would bear it no longer. He knew well enough what duties he owed the queen as an earl and grand marshal of England, but he did not understand being cuffed and beaten like a menial servant; and that his body suffered in every part from the blow he had received."

His resentment, however, got soothed and softened in time, and he was again admitted to favor, though the consequences of such quarrels are seldom fully repaired. The reconciliation was, however, in this case, apparently complete, and in the following year Essex was himself appointed the Governor, or, as styled in those days, the Lord Deputy of Ireland.

He went to his province, and took command of the forces which had been collected there, and engaged zealously in the work of suppressing the rebellion. For some reason or other, however, he made very little progress. The name of the leader of the rebels was the Earl of Tyrone.[D] Tyrone wanted a parley, but did not dare to trust himself in Essex's power. It was at last, however, agreed that the two leaders should come down to a river, one of them upon each side, and talk across it, neither general to have any troops or attendants with him. This plan was carried into effect. Essex, stationing a troop near him, on a hill, rode down to the water on one side, while Tyrone came into the river as far as his horse could wade on the other, and then the two earls attempted to negotiate terms of peace by shouting across the current of the stream.

[Footnote D: Spelled in the old histories Tir-Oen.]

Nothing effectual was accomplished by this and some other similar parleys, and in the mean time the weeks were passing away, and little was done toward suppressing the rebellion. The queen was dissatisfied. She sent Essex letters of complaint and censure. These letters awakened the lord deputy's resentment. The breach was thus rapidly widening, when Essex all at once conceived the idea of going himself to England, without permission, and without giving any notice of his intention, to endeavor, by a personal interview, to reinstate himself in the favor of the queen.

This was a very bold step. It was entirely contrary to military etiquette for an officer to leave his command and go home to his sovereign without orders and without permission. The plan, however, might have succeeded. Leicester did once succeed in such a measure; but in this case, unfortunately, it failed. Essex traveled with the utmost dispatch, crossed the Channel, made the best of his way to the palace where the queen was then residing, and pressed through the opposition of all the attendants into the queen's private apartment, in his traveling dress, soiled and way-worn. The queen was at her toilet, with her hair down over her eyes. Essex fell on his knees before her, kissed her hand, and made great professions of gratitude and love, and of an extreme desire to deserve and enjoy her favor. The queen was astonished at his appearance, but Essex thought that she received him kindly. He went away after a short interview, greatly pleased with the prospect of a favorable issue to the desperate step he had taken. His joy, however, was soon dispelled. In the course of the day he was arrested by order of the queen, and sent to his house under the custody of an officer. He had presumed too far.

Essex was kept thus secluded and confined for some time. His house was on the bank of the river. None of his friends, not even his countess, were allowed access to him. His impetuous spirit wore itself out in chafing against the restraints and means of coercion which were pressing upon him; but he would not submit. The mind of the queen, too, was deeply agitated all the time by that most tempestuous of all mental conflicts, a struggle between resentment and love. Her affection for her proud-spirited favorite seemed as strong as ever, but she was determined to make him yield in the contest she had commenced with him. How often cases precisely similar occur in less conspicuous scenes of action, where they who love each other with a sincere and uncontrollable affection take their stand in attitudes of hostility, each determined that the obstinacy of the other shall give way, and each heart persisting in its own determination, resentment and love struggling all the time in a dreadful contest, which keeps the soul in a perpetual commotion, and allows of no peace till either the obstinacy yields or the love is extinguished and gone.

It was indirectly made known to Essex that if he would confess his fault, ask the queen's forgiveness, and petition for a release from confinement, in order that he might return to his duties in Ireland, the difficulty could be settled. But no, he would make no concessions. The queen, in retaliation, increased the pressure upon him. The more strongly he felt the pressure, the more his proud and resentful spirit was aroused. He walked his room, his soul boiling with anger and chagrin, while the queen, equally distressed and harassed by the conflict in her own soul, still persevered, hoping every day that the unbending spirit with which she was contending would yield at last.

At length the tidings came to her that Essex, worn out with agitation and suffering, was seriously sick. The historians doubt whether his sickness was real or feigned; but there is not much difficulty in understanding, from the circumstances of the case, what its real nature was. Such mental conflicts as those which he endured suspend the powers of digestion and accelerate the pulsations of the heart, which beats in the bosom with a preternatural frequency and force, like a bird fluttering to get free from a snare. The result is a sort of fever burning slowly in the veins, and an emaciation which wastes the strength away, and, in impetuous and uncontrollable spirits, like that of Essex, sometimes exhausts the powers of life altogether. The sickness, therefore, though of mental origin, becomes bodily and real; but then the sufferer is often ready, in such cases, to add a little to it by feigning. An instinct teaches him that nothing is so likely to move the heart whose cruelty causes him to suffer, as a knowledge of the extreme to which it has reduced him. Essex was doubtless willing that Elizabeth should know that he was sick. Her knowing it had, in some measure, the usual effect. It reawakened and strengthened the love she had felt for him, but did not give it absolutely the victory. She sent eightphysicians to him, to examine and consult upon his case. She caused some broth to be made for him, and gave it to one of these physicians to carry to him, directing the messenger, in a faltering voice, to say to Essex that if it were proper to do so she would have come to see him herself. She then turned away to hide her tears. Strange inconsistency of the human heart--resentment and anger holding their ground in the soul against the object of such deep and unconquerable love. It would be incredible, were it not that probably every single one of all the thousands who may read this story has experienced the same.

Nothing has so great an effect in awakening in the heart a strong sentiment of kindness as the performance of a kind act. Feeling originates and controls action, it is true, but then, on the other hand, action has a prodigious power in modifying feeling. Elizabeth's acts of kindness to Essex in his sickness produced a renewal of her tenderness for him so strong that her obstinacy and anger gave way before it, and she soon began to desire some mode of releasing him from his confinement, and restoring him to favor. Essex was softened too. In a word, there was finally a reconciliation, though it was accomplished by slow degrees, and by means of a sort of series of capitulations. There was an investigation of his case before the privy council, which resulted in a condemnation of his conduct, and a recommendation to the mercy of the queen; and then followed some communications between Essex and his sovereign, in which he expressed sorrow for his faults, and made satisfactory promises for the future.

The queen, however, had not magnanimity enough to let the quarrel end without taunting and irritating the penitent with expressions of triumph. In reply to his acknowledgments and professions, she told him that she was glad to hear of his good intentions, and she hoped that he would show, by his future conduct, that he meant to fulfill them; that he had tried her patience for a long time, but she hoped that henceforth she should have no further trouble. If it had been her father, she added, instead of herself, that he had had to deal with, he would not have been pardoned at all. It could not be a very cordial reconciliation which was consummated by such words as these. But it was very like Elizabeth to utter them. They who are governed by their temper are governed by it even in their love.

Essex was not restored to office. In fact, he did not wish to be restored. He said that he was resolved henceforth to lead a private life. But even in respect to this plan he was at the mercy of the queen, for his private income was in a great measure derived from a monopoly, as it is called, in a certain kind of wines, which had been granted to him some time before. It was a very customary mode, in those days, of enriching favorites, to grant them monopolies of certain kinds of merchandise, that is, the exclusive right to sell them. The persons to whom this privilege was granted would underlet their right to merchants in various parts of the kingdom, on condition of receiving a certain share of the profits. Essex had thus derived a great revenue from his monopoly of wines. The grant, however, was expiring, and he petitioned the queen that it might be renewed.

The interest which Essex felt in the renewal of this grant was one of the strongest inducements to lead him to submit to the humiliations which he had endured, and to make concessions to the queen. But he was disappointed in his hopes. The queen, elated a little with the triumph already attained, and, perhaps, desirous of the pleasure of humbling Essex still more, refused at present to renew his monopoly, saying that she thought it would do him good to be restricted a little, for a time, in his means. "Unmanageable beasts," she said, "had to be tamed by being stinted in their provender."

Essex was sharply stung by such a refusal, accompanied, too, by such an insult. He was full of indignation and anger. At first he gave free expression to his feelings of vexation in conversation with those around him. The queen, he said, had got to be a perverse and obstinate old woman, as crooked in mind as she was in body. He had plenty of enemies to listen to these speeches, and to report them in such a way as that they should reach the queen. A new breach was consequently opened, which seemed now wider than ever, and irreparable.

At least it seemed so to Essex; and, abandoning all plans for again enjoying the favor of Elizabeth, he began to consider what he could do to undermine her power and rise upon the ruins of it. The idea was insanity, but passion always makes men insane. James, king of Scotland, the son and successor of Mary, was the rightful heir to the English throne after Elizabeth's death. In order to make his right of succession more secure, he had wished to have Elizabeth acknowledge it; but she, always dreading terribly the thoughts of death, could never bear to think of a successor, and seemed to hate every one who entertained any expectation of following her. Essex suppressed all outward expressions of violence and anger; became thoughtful, moody, and sullen; held secret consultations with desperate intriguers, and finally formed a scheme to organize a rebellion, to bring King James's troops to England to support it, to take possession of the Tower and of the strong-holds about London, to seize the palace of the queen, overturn her government, and compel her both to acknowledge James's right to the succession and to restore Essex himself to power.

The personal character of Essex had given him a very wide-spread popularity and influence, and he had, consequently, very extensive materials at his command for organizing a powerful conspiracy. The plot was gradually matured, extending itself, in the course of the few following months, not only throughout England, but also into France and Spain. The time for the final explosion was drawing near, when, as usual in such cases, intelligence of the existence of this treason, in the form of vague rumors, reached the queen. One day, when the leading conspirators were assembled at Essex's palace, a messenger came to summon the earl to appear before the council. They received, also, private intelligence that their plots were probably discovered. While they were considering what to do in this emergency--all in a state of great perplexity and fear--a person came, pretending to be a deputy sent from some of the principal citizens of London, to say to Essex that they were ready to espouse his cause. Essex immediately became urgent to commence the insurrection at once. Some of his friends, on the other hand, were in favor of abandoning the enterprise, and flying from the country; but Essex said he had rather be shot at the head of his bands, than to wander all his days beyond the seas, a fugitive and a vagabond.

The conspirators acceded to their leader's councils. They sent word, accordingly, into the city, and began to make their arrangements to rise in arms the next morning. The night was spent in anxious preparations. Early in the morning, a deputation of some of the highest officers of the government, with a train of attendants, came to Essex's palace, and demanded entrance in the name of the queen. The gates of the palace were shut and guarded. At last, after some hesitation and delay, the conspirators opened a wicket, that is, a small gate within the large one, which would admit one person at a time. They allowed the officers themselves to enter, but shut the gate immediately so as to exclude the attendants. The officers found themselves in a large court-yard filled with armed men, Essex standing calmly at the head of them. They demanded what was the meaning of such an unusual assemblage. Essex replied that it was to defend his life from conspiracies formed against it by his enemies. The officers denied this danger, and began to expostulate with Essex in angry terms, and the attendants on his side to reply with vociferations and threats, when Essex, to end the altercation, took the officers into the palace. He conducted them to a room and shut them up, to keep them as hostages.

It was now near ten o'clock, and, leaving his prisoners in their apartment, under a proper guard, Essex sallied forth, with the more resolute and desperate of his followers, and proceeded into the city, to bring out into action the forces which he supposed were ready to co-operate with him there. He rode on through the streets, calling to arms, and shouting, "For the queen! For the queen!" His design was to convey the impression that the movement which he was making was not against the queen herself, but against his own enemies in her councils, and that she was herself on his side. The people of London, however, could not be so easily deceived. The mayor had received warning before, from the council, to be ready to suppress the movement, if one should be made. As soon, therefore, as Essex and his company were fairly in the city, the gates were shut and barred to prevent his return. One of the queen's principal ministers of state too, at the head of a small troop of horsemen, came in and rode through the streets, proclaiming Essex a traitor, and calling upon all the citizens to aid in arresting him. One of Essex's followers fired a pistol at this officer to stop his proclamation, but the people generally seemed disposed to listen to him, and to comply with his demand. After riding, therefore, through some of the principal streets, he returned to the queen, and reported to her that all was well in the city; there was no danger that Essex would succeed in raising a rebellion there.

In the mean time, the further Essex proceeded, the more he found himself environed with difficulties and dangers. The people began to assemble here and there with evident intent to impede his movements. They blocked up the streets with carts and coaches to prevent his escape. His followers, one after another, finding all hope of success gone, abandoned their despairing leader and fled. Essex himself, with the few who still adhered to him, wandered about till two o'clock, finding the way of retreat every where hemmed up against him.

At length he fled to the river side, took a boat, with the few who still remained with him, and ordered the watermen to row as rapidly as possible up the river. They landed at Westminster, retreated to Essex's house, fled into it with the utmost precipitation, and barricaded the doors. Essex himself was excited in the highest degree, fully determined to die there rather than surrender himself a prisoner. The terrible desperation to which men are reduced in emergencies like these is shown by the fact that one of his followers did actually station himself at a window bare-headed, inviting a shot from the pistols of the pursuers, who had by this time environed the house, and were preparing to force their way in. His plan succeeded. He was shot, and died that night.

Essex himself was not quite so desperate as this. He soon saw, however, that he must sooner or later yield. He could not stand a siege in his own private dwelling against the whole force of the English realm. He surrendered about six in the evening, and was sent to the Tower. He was soon afterward brought to trial. The facts, with all the arrangements and details of the conspiracy, were fully proved, and he was condemned to die.

As the unhappy prisoner lay in his gloomy dungeon in the Tower, the insane excitement under which he had for so many months been acting slowly ebbed away. He awoke from it gradually, as one recovers his senses after a dreadful dream. He saw how utterly irretrievable was the mischief which had been done. Remorse for his guilt in having attempted to destroy the peace of the kingdom to gratify his own personal feelings of revenge; recollections of the favors which Elizabeth had shown him, and of the love which she had felt for him, obviously so deep and sincere; the consciousness that his life was fairly forfeited, and that he must die--to lie in his cell and think of these things, overwhelmed him with anguish and despair. The brilliant prospects which were so recently before him were all forever gone, leaving nothing in their place but the grim phantom of an executioner, standing with an ax by the side of a dreadful platform, with a block upon it, half revealed and half hidden by the black cloth which covered it like a pall.

Elizabeth, in her palace, was in a state of mind scarcely less distressing than that of the wretched prisoner in his cell. The old conflict was renewed--pride and resentment on the one side, and love which would not be extinguished on the other. If Essex would sue for pardon, she would remit his sentence and allow him to live. Why would he not do it? If he would send her the ring which she had given him for exactly such an emergency, he might be saved. Why did he not send it? The courtiers and statesmen about her urged her to sign the warrant; the peace of the country demanded the execution of the laws in a case of such unquestionable guilt. They told her, too, that Essex wished to die, that he knew that he was hopelessly and irretrievably ruined, and that life, if granted to him, was a boon which would compromise her own safety and confer no benefit on him. Still Elizabeth waited and waited in an agony of suspense, in hopes that the ring would come; the sending of it would be so far an act of submission on his part as would put it in her power to do the rest. Her love could bend her pride, indomitable as it usually was, almost to the whole concession, but it would not give up quite all. It demanded some sacrifice on his part, which sacrifice the sending of the ring would have rendered. The ring did not come, nor any petition for mercy, and at length the fatal warrant was signed.

What the courtiers said about Essex's desire to die was doubtless true. Like every other person involved in irretrievable sufferings and sorrows, he wanted to live, and he wanted to die. The two contradictory desires shared dominion in his heart, sometimes struggling together in a tumultuous conflict, and sometimes reigning in alternation, in calms more terrible, in fact, than the tempests which preceded and followed them.

At the appointed time the unhappy man was led out to the court-yard in the Tower where the last scene was to be enacted. The lieutenant of the Tower presided, dressed in a black velvet gown, over a suit of black satin. The "scaffold" was a platform about twelve feet square and four feet high, with a railing around it, and steps by which to ascend. The block was in the center of it, covered, as well as the platform itself, with black cloth. There were seats erected near for those who were appointed to be present at the execution. Essex ascended the platform with a firm step, and, surveying the solemn scene around him with calmness and composure, he began to speak.

He asked the forgiveness of God, of the spectators present, and of the queen, for the crimes for which he was about to suffer. He acknowledged his guilt, and the justice of his condemnation. His mind seemed deeply imbued with a sense of his accountability to God, and he expressed a strong desire to be forgiven, for Christ's sake, for all the sins which he had committed, which had been, he said, most numerous and aggravated from his earliest years. He asked the spectators present to join him in his devotions, and he then proceeded to offer a short prayer, in which he implored pardon for his sins, and a long life and happy reign for the queen. The prayer ended, all was ready. The executioner, according to the strange custom on such occasions, then asked his pardon for the violence which he was about to commit, which Essex readily granted. Essex laid his head upon the block, and it required three blows to complete its severance from the body. When the deed was done, the executioner took up the bleeding head, saying solemnly, as he held it, "God save the queen."

There were but few spectators present at this dreadful scene, and they were chiefly persons required to attend in the discharge of their official duties. There was, however, one exception; it was that of a courtier of high rank, who had long been Essex's inveterate enemy, and who could not deny himself the savage pleasure of witnessing his rival's destruction. But even the stern and iron-hearted officers of the Tower were shocked at his appearing at the scaffold. They urged him to go away, and not distress the dying man by his presence at such an hour. The courtier yielded so far as to withdraw from the scaffold; but he could not go far away. He found a place where he could stand unobserved to witness the scene, at the window of a turret which overlooked the court-yard.

CHAPTER XII.

THE CONCLUSION.

1600-1603

Question of Essex's guilt.--General opinion of mankind.--Elizabeth's distress.--Fall of Essex's party.--Wounds of the heart.--Elizabeth's efforts to recover her spirits.--Embassage from France.--A conversation.--Thoughts of Essex.--Harrington.--The Countess of Nottingham.--The ring.--The Countess of Nottingham's confession.--The queen's indignation.--Bitter reminiscences.--The queen removes to Richmond.--Elizabeth grows worse.--The private chapel and the closets.--The wedding ring.--The queen's friends abandon her.--The queen's voice fails.--She calls her council together.--The chaplains.--The prayers.--The queen's death.--King James proclaimed.--Portrait of James the First.--Burial of the queen.--Westminster Abbey.--Its history.--The Poet's Corner.--Henry the Seventh's Chapel.--Elizabeth's monument.--James.--Mary's monument.--Feelings of visitors.--Summary of Elizabeth's character.

There can be no doubt that Essex was really guilty of the treason for which he was condemned, but mankind have generally been inclined to consider Elizabeth rather than him as the one really accountable, both for the crime and its consequences. To elate and intoxicate, in the first place, an ardent and ambitious boy, by flattery and favors, and then, in the end, on the occurrence of real or fancied causes of displeasure, to tease and torment so sensitive and impetuous a spirit to absolute madness and phrensy, was to take the responsibility, in a great measure, for all the effects which might follow. At least so it has generally been regarded. By almost all the readers of the story, Essex is pitied and mourned--it is Elizabeth that is condemned. It is a melancholy story; but scenes exactly parallel to this case are continually occurring in private life all around us, where sorrows and sufferings which are, so far as the heart is concerned, precisely the same result from the combined action, or rather, perhaps, the alternating and contending action, of fondness, passion, and obstinacy. The results are always, in their own nature, the same, though not often on so great a scale as to make the wrong which follows treason against a realm, and the consequences a beheading in the Tower.

There must have been some vague consciousness of this her share in the guilt of the transaction in Elizabeth's mind, even while the trial of Essex was going on. We know that she was harassed by the most tormenting suspense and perplexity while the question of the execution of his sentence was pending. Of course, when the plot was discovered, Essex's party and all his friends fell immediately from all influence and consideration at court. Many of them were arrested and imprisoned, and four were executed, as he had been. The party which had been opposed to him acquired at once the entire ascendency, and they all, judges, counselors, statesmen, and generals, combined their influence to press upon the queen the necessity of his execution. She signed one warrant and delivered it to the officer; but then, as soon as the deed was done, she was so overwhelmed with distress and anguish that she sent to recall it, and had it canceled. Finally she signed another, and the sentence was executed.

Time will cure, in our earlier years, most of the sufferings, and calm most of the agitations of the soul, however incurable and uncontrollable they may at first appear to the sufferer. But in the later periods of life, when severe shocks strike very heavily upon the soul, there is found far less of buoyancy and recovering power to meet the blow. In such cases the stunned and bewildered spirit moves on, after receiving its wound, staggering, as it were, with faintness and pain, and leaving it for a long time uncertain whether it will ultimately rise and recover, or sink down and die.

Dreadfully wounded as Elizabeth was, in all the inmost feelings and affections of her heart, by the execution of her beloved favorite, she was a woman of far too much spirit and energy to yield without a struggle. She made the greatest efforts possible after his death to banish the subject from her mind, and to recover her wonted spirits. She went on hunting excursions and parties of pleasure. She prosecuted with great energy her war with the Spaniards, and tried to interest herself in the siege and defense of Continental cities. She received an embassage from the court of France with great pomp and parade, and made a grand progress through a part of her dominions, with a long train of attendants, to the house of a nobleman, where she entertained the embassador many days in magnificent state, at her own expense, with plate and furniture brought from her own palaces for the purpose. She even planned an interview between herself and the King of France, and went to Dover to effect it.

But all would not do. Nothing could drive the thoughts of Essex from her mind, or dispel the dejection with which the recollection of her love for him, and of his unhappy fate, oppressed her spirit. A year or two passed away, but time brought no relief. Sometimes she was fretful and peevish, and sometimes hopelessly dejected and sad. She told the French embassador one day that she was weary of her life, and when she attempted to speak of Essex as the cause of her grief, she sighed bitterly and burst into tears.

When she recovered her composure, she told the embassador that she had always been uneasy about Essex while he lived, and, knowing his impetuosity of spirit and his ambition, she had been afraid that he would one day attempt something which would compromise his life, and she had warned and entreated him not to be led into any such designs, for, if he did so, his fate would have to be decided by the stern authority of law, and not by her own indulgent feelings but that all her earnest warnings had been insufficient to save him.

It was the same whenever any thing occurred which recalled thoughts of Essex to her mind; it almost always brought tears to her eyes. When Essex was commanding in Ireland, it will be recollected that he had, on one occasion, come to a parley with Tyrone, the rebel leader, across the current of a stream. An officer in his army, named Harrington, had been with him on this occasion, and present, though at a little distance, during the interview. After Essex had left Ireland, another lord-deputy had been appointed; but the rebellion continued to give the government a great deal of trouble. The Spaniards came over to Tyrone's assistance, and Elizabeth's mind was much occupied with plans for subduing him. One day Harrington was at court in the presence of the queen, and she asked him if he had ever seen Tyrone. Harrington replied that he had. The queen then recollected the former interview which Harrington had had with him, and she said, "Oh, now I recollect that you have seen him before!" This thought recalled Essex so forcibly to her mind, and filled her with such painful emotions, that she looked up to Harrington with a countenance full of grief: tears came to her eyes, and she beat her breast with every indication of extreme mental suffering.

Things went on in this way until toward the close of 1602, when an incident occurred which seemed to strike down at once and forever what little strength and spirit the queen had remaining. The Countess of Nottingham, a celebrated lady of the court, was dangerously sick, and had sent for the queen to come and see her, saying that she had a communication to make to her majesty herself, personally, which she was very anxious to make to her before she died. The queen went accordingly to see her.

When she arrived at the bedside the countess showed her a ring. Elizabeth immediately recognized it as the ring which she had given to Essex, and which she had promised to consider a special pledge of her protection, and which was to be sent to her by him whenever he found himself in any extremity of danger and distress. The queen eagerly demanded where it came from. The countess replied that Essex had sent the ring to her during his imprisonment in the Tower, and after his condemnation, with an earnest request that she would deliver it to the queen as the token of her promise of protection, and of his own supplication for mercy. The countess added that she had intended to deliver the ring according to Essex's request, but her husband, who was the unhappy prisoner's enemy, forbade her to do it; that ever since the execution of Essex she had been greatly distressed at the consequences of her having withheld the ring; and that now, as she was about to leave the world herself, she felt that she could not die in peace without first seeing the queen, and acknowledging fully what she had done, and imploring her forgiveness.

The queen was thrown into a state of extreme indignation and displeasure by this statement. She reproached the dying countess in the bitterest terms, and shook her as she lay helpless in her bed, saying, "God may forgive you if he pleases, but I_ never will!" She then went away in a rage.

Her exasperation, however, against the countess was soon succeeded by bursts of inconsolable grief at the recollection of the hopeless and irretrievable loss of the object of her affection whose image the ring called back so forcibly to her mind. Her imagination wandered in wretchedness and despair to the gloomy dungeon in the Tower where Essex had been confined, and painted him pining there, day after day, in dreadful suspense and anxiety, waiting for her to redeem the solemn pledge by which she had bound herself in giving him the ring. All the sorrow which she had felt at his untimely and cruel fate was awakened afresh, and became more poignant than ever. She made them place cushions for her upon the floor, in the most inner and secluded of her apartments, and there she would lie all the day long, her hair disheveled, her dress neglected, her food refused, and her mind a prey to almost uninterrupted anguish and grief.

In January, 1603, she felt that she was drawing toward her end, and she decided to be removed from Westminster to Richmond, because there was there an arrangement of closets communicating with her chamber, in which she could easily and conveniently attend divine service. She felt that she had now done with the world, and all the relief and comfort which she could find at all from the pressure of her distress was in that sense of protection and safety which she experienced when in the presence of God and listening to the exercises of devotion.

It was a cold and stormy day in January when she went to Richmond; but, being restless and ill at ease, she would not be deterred by that circumstance from making the journey. She became worse after this removal. She made them put cushions again for her upon the floor, and she would lie upon them all the day, refusing to go to her bed. There was a communication from her chamber to closets connected with a chapel, where she had been accustomed to sit and hear divine service. These closets were of the form of small galleries, where the queen and her immediate attendants could sit. There was one open and public; another--a smaller one--was private, with curtains which could be drawn before it, so as to screen those within from the notice of the congregation. The queen intended, first, to go into the great closet; but, feeling too weak for this, she changed her mind, and ordered the private one to be prepared. At last she decided not to attempt to make even this effort, but ordered the cushions to be put down upon the floor, near the entrance, in her own room, and she lay there while the prayers were read, listening to the voice of the clergyman as it came in to her through the open door.

One day she asked them to take off the wedding ring with which she had commemorated her espousal to her kingdom and her people on the day of her coronation. The flesh had swollen around it so that it could not be removed. The attendants procured an instrument and cut it in two, and so relieved the finger from the pressure. The work was done in silence and solemnity, the queen herself, as well as the attendants, regarding it as a symbol that the union, of which the ring had been the pledge, was about to be sundered forever.

She sunk rapidly day by day, and, as it became more and more probable that she would soon cease to live, the nobles and statesmen who had been attendants at her court for so many years withdrew one after another from the palace, and left London secretly, but with eager dispatch, to make their way to Scotland, in order to be the first to hail King James, the moment they should learn that Elizabeth had ceased to breathe.

Her being abandoned thus by these heartless friends did not escape the notice of the dying queen. Though her strength of body was almost gone, the soul was as active and busy as ever within its failing tenement. She watched every thing--noticed every thing, growing more and more jealous and irritable just in proportion as her situation became helpless and forlorn. Every thing seemed to conspire to deepen the despondency and gloom which darkened her dying hours.

Her strength rapidly declined. Her voice grew fainter and fainter, until, on the 23d of March, she could no longer speak. In the afternoon of that day she aroused herself a little, and contrived to make signs to have her council called to her bedside. Those who had not gone to Scotland came. They asked her whom she wished to have succeed her on the throne. She could not answer, but when they named King James of Scotland, she made a sign of assent. After a time the counselors went away.

At six o'clock in the evening she made signs for the archbishop and her chaplains to come to her. They were sent for and came. When they came in, they approached her bedside and kneeled. The patient was lying upon her back speechless, but her eye, still moving watchfully and observing every thing, showed that the faculties of the soul were unimpaired. One of the clergymen asked her questions respecting her faith. Of course, she could not answer in words. She made signs, however, with her eyes and her hands, which seemed to prove that she had full possession of all her faculties. The by-standers looked on with breathless attention. The aged bishop, who had asked the questions, then began to pray for her. He continued his prayer a long time, and then pronouncing a benediction upon her, he was about to rise, but she made a sign. The bishop did not understand what she meant, but a lady present said that she wished the bishop to continue his devotions. The bishop, though weary with kneeling, continued his prayer half an hour longer. He then closed again, but she repeated the sign. The bishop, finding thus that his ministrations gave her so much comfort, renewed them with greater fervency than before, and continued his supplications for a long time--so long, that those who had been present at the commencement of the service went away softly, one after another, so that when at last the bishop retired, the queen was left with her nurses and her women alone. These attendants remained at their dying sovereign's bedside for a few hours longer, watching the failing pulse, the quickened breathing, and all the other indications of approaching dissolution. As hour after hour thus passed on, they wished that their weary task was done, and that both their patient and themselves were at rest. This lasted till midnight, and then the intelligence was communicated about the palace that Elizabeth was no more.

In the mean time all the roads to Scotland were covered, as it were, with eager aspirants for the favor of the distinguished personage, there, who, from the instant Elizabeth ceased to breathe, became King of England. They flocked into Scotland by sea and by land, urging their way as rapidly as possible, each eager to be foremost in paying his homage to the rising sun. The council assembled and proclaimed King James. Elizabeth lay neglected and forgotten. The interest she had inspired was awakened only by her power, and that being gone, nobody mourned for her, or lamented her death. The attention of the kingdom was soon universally absorbed in the plans for receiving and proclaiming the new monarch from the North, and in anticipations of the splendid pageantry which was to signalize his taking his seat upon the English throne.

In due time the body of the deceased queen was deposited with those of its progenitors, in the ancient place of sepulture of the English kings, Westminster Abbey. Westminster Abbey, in the sense in which that term is used in history, is not to be conceived of as a building, nor even as a group of buildings, but rather as a long succession of buildings like a dynasty following each other in a line, the various structures having been renewed and rebuilt constantly, as parts or wholes decayed, from century to century, for twelve or fifteen hundred years. The spot received its consecration at a very early day. It was then an island formed by the waters of a little tributary to the Thames, which has long since entirely disappeared. Written records of its sacredness, and of the sacred structures which have occupied it, go back more than a thousand years, and beyond that time tradition mounts still further, carrying the consecration of the spot almost to the Christian era, by telling us that the Apostle Peter himself, in his missionary wanderings, had a chapel or an oratory there.

The spot has been, in all ages, the great burial-place of the English kings, whose monuments and effigies adorn its walls and aisles in endless variety. A vast number, too, of the statesmen, generals, and naval heroes of the British empire have been admitted to the honor of having their remains deposited under its marble floor. Even literary genius has a little corner assigned it--the mighty aristocracy whose mortal remains it is the main function of the building to protect having so far condescended toward intellectual greatness as to allow to Milton, Addison, and Shakspeare modest monuments behind a door. The place is called the Poets' Corner; and so famed and celebrated is this vast edifice every where, that the phrase by which even this obscure and insignificant portion of it is known is familiar to every ear and every tongue throughout the English world.

The body of Elizabeth was interred in a part of the edifice called Henry the Seventh's Chapel. The word chapel, in the European sense, denotes ordinarily a subordinate edifice connected with the main body of a church, and opening into it. Most frequently, in fact, a chapel is a mere recess or alcove, separated from the area of the church by a small screen or gilded iron railing. In the Catholic churches these chapels are ornamented with sculptures and paintings, with altars and crucifixes, and other such furniture. Sometimes they are built expressly as monumental structures, in which case they are often of considerable size, and are ornamented with great magnificence and splendor. This was the case with Henry the Seventh's Chapel. The whole building is, in fact his tomb. Vast sums were expended in the construction of it, the work of which extended through two reigns. It is now one of the most attractive portions of the great pile which it adorns. Elizabeth's body was deposited here, and here her monument was erected.

It will be recollected that James, who now succeeded Elizabeth, was the son of Mary Queen of Scots. Soon after his accession to the throne, he removed the remains of his mother from their place of sepulture near the scene of her execution, and interred them in the south aisle of Henry the Seventh's Chapel, while the body of Elizabeth occupied the northern one.[E] He placed, also, over Mary's remains, a tomb very similar in its plan and design to that by which the memory of Elizabeth was honored; and there the rival queens have since reposed in silence and peace under the same paved floor. And though the monuments do not materially differ in their architectural forms, it is found that the visitors who go continually to the spot gaze with a brief though lively interest at the one, while they linger long and mournfully over the other.

[Footnote E: See our history of Mary Queen of Scots, near the close. Aisles in English Cathedral churches are colonnades, or spaces between columns on an open floor, and not passages between pews, as with us. In monumental churches like Westminster Abbey there are no pews.]

* * * * *

The character of Elizabeth has not generally awakened among mankind much commendation or sympathy. They who censure or condemn her should, however, reflect how very conspicuous was the stage on which she acted, and how minutely all her faults have been paraded to the world. That she deserved the reproaches which have been so freely cast upon her memory can not be denied. It will moderate, however, any tendency to censoriousness in our mode of uttering them, if we consider to how little advantage we should ourselves appear, if all the words of fretfulness and irritability which we have ever spoken, all our insincerity and double-dealing, our selfishness, our pride, our petty resentments, our caprice, and our countless follies, were exposed as fully to the public gaze as were those of this renowned and glorious, but unhappy queen.

THE END.

Made in United States
Troutdale, OR
10/24/2024